"Written with the sensitivit
scientist, this book provide
guide for families faced wi
the best treatments for th
given a practical framework and vocabulary to critically
evaluate their options and ensure that the methods they
choose are sound and will provide their child with the best
opportunity for success."

—Cassandra R. Newsom, PsyD, Licensed Clinical Psychologist,
Assistant Professor of Pediatrics, Psychiatry, and Psychology,
Vanderbilt University Medical School, and Director of
Psychology Education, Treatment and Research Institute for
Autism Spectrum Disorders, Vanderbilt Kennedy Center

"Families of individuals with an autism spectrum disorder are
bombarded with countless accounts of effective treatments
for autism. *A Brief Guide to Autism Treatments* provides parents
and caregivers with reliable and useful information that will
allow them to make educated decisions regarding treatment
for their loved one on the autism spectrum."

—Hanna C. Rue, PhD, BCBA-D, Executive
Director, National Autism Center

"*A Brief Guide to Autism Treatments* provides families with
a user-friendly introductory guide to current treatments
for autism. The emphasis on scientific evidence will help
provide guidance in making informed decisions for a very
challenging disorder."

—Lauren Cyd Solotar, PhD, ABPP, CEO, May Institute

"In the ever-growing complexity of treatments for children with ASD, Sandberg and Spritz's timely volume offers a thoughtful, concise, and accessible analysis of available interventions that will help parents and families negotiate the confusion and separate the wheat from the chaff."

—*Keith A. Crnic, PhD, Professor and Chair, Department of Psychology, Arizona State University*

"Carefully investigated and concisely written, Sandberg and Spritz have provided for the first time an extremely well-researched and accessible guide on available treatments for children with autism spectrum disorders. Families with an autistic child are confronted with the overwhelming task of finding the best interventions for their child amidst a dizzying array of information from professionals and educators, other families, printed materials, and the internet. The process of sorting through this information is daunting, confusing, and extremely time-consuming, making it nearly impossible for families with a special needs child to gain the critical insights they need. The authors not only describe the treatments available and their costs, they provide a well-rounded assessment of the support for any given intervention, from online information to parent testimonials to hard scientific evidence. This book will become the definitive treatment resource guide for all families of children with autism and I strongly recommend it to anyone committed to optimizing interventions for children with autism spectrum disorders."

—*Katherine M. Martien, MD, Neurodevelopmental Pediatrics Specialist Massachusetts General Hospital Instructor, Harvard Medical School*

A BRIEF GUIDE TO

AUTISM

TREATMENTS

of related interest

The Complete Guide to Asperger's Syndrome
Tony Attwood
ISBN 978 1 84310 495 7 (hardback)
ISBN 978 1 84310 669 2 (paperback)
eISBN 978 1 84642 559 2

Understanding Applied Behavior Analysis
An Introduction to ABA for Parents, Teachers, and other Professionals
Albert J. Kearney
ISBN 978 1 84310 860 3
eISBN 978 1 84642 726 8
Part of the JKP Essentials series

Dietary Interventions in Autism Spectrum Disorders
Why They Work When They Do, Why They Don't When They Don't
Kenneth J. Aitken
ISBN 978 1 84310 939 6
eISBN 978 1 84642 860 9

Understanding Controversial Therapies for Children with Autism, Attention Deficit Disorder and Other Learning Disabilities
A Guide to Complementary and Alternative Medicine
Lisa A. Kurtz
ISBN 978 1 84310 864 1
eISBN 978 1 84642 761 9
Part of the JKP Essentials series

The Miller Method®
Developing the Capacities of Children on the Autism Spectrum
Arnold Miller
With Kristina Chrétien
ISBN 978 1 84310 722 4
eISBN 978 1 84642 583 7

ELISABETH HOLLISTER SANDBERG
AND BECKY L. SPRITZ

A BRIEF GUIDE TO
AUTISM
TREATMENTS

Jessica Kingsley *Publishers*
London and Philadelphia

First published in 2013
by Jessica Kingsley Publishers
116 Pentonville Road
London N1 9JB, UK
and
400 Market Street, Suite 400
Philadelphia, PA 19106, USA

www.jkp.com

Library of Congress Cataloging in Publication Data
Sandberg, Elisabeth Hollister.
 A brief guide to autism treatments / Elisabeth Hollister Sandberg and Becky L. Spritz.
  p. cm.
 Includes bibliographical references and index.
 ISBN 978-1-84905-904-6 (alk. paper) -- ISBN 978-0-85700-650-9 1. Autism in children--Treatment. 2.
Autistic children--Care. I. Spritz, Becky L. II. Title.
 RJ506.A9S26 2013
 618.92'85882--dc23
                            2012024418

British Library Cataloguing in Publication Data
A CIP catalogue record for this book is available from the British Library

ISBN 978 1 84905 904 6
eISBN 978 0 85700 650 9

Printed and bound in Great Britain

We dedicate this book to all of the other parents who have needed help making choices.

Acknowledgments

We owe many thanks to many people for making this book possible, but two sources of inspiration demand explicit gratitude:

EHS thanks the doctoral students in her Autism in Context Seminar at Suffolk University in Boston. This book grew from a project focused on uniting science with clinical practice in ways that are genuinely connected to the challenges that families face.

BLS thanks Mr. Matthias Brown and the community of Petersfield, Jamaica for reminding her that autism is a global problem, and that in spite of all we know about autism, there is more that we don't.

Contents

Notes

INTERNATIONAL CAVEAT

We, the authors, live and work in the United States. As such, our coverage is necessarily Amerocentric. The vast majority of what we report applies in other countries, but our international readers may find that access, legality, availability and licensure are different in their home countries. We occasionally make reference to the US Food and Drug Administration (FDA), which, in the United States, is the gatekeeper for all things medical. The FDA is generally recognized as being more stringent than the equivalent regulatory bodies in many other nations. Also, our cost estimates are reported in US dollars.

FEEDBACK

Undoubtedly, we will have readers who would like to draw our attention to additional evidence, or who would like to lobby for the inclusion of additional topics. We invite suggestions that might guide and shape future editions of this book. Please send such correspondence via email to AutismTreatmentBook@gmail.com

1 ABOUT THIS BOOK

Elisabeth Hollister Sandberg
and Becky L. Spritz

WHAT IS THE AUTISM SPECTRUM?

If you are reading this book you probably have or know a child with an autism spectrum disorder (ASD). We will not go into the details of diagnosis except to say that autism is a neurologically based developmental disorder characterized by deficits in the domains of communication, social interaction and behavior. Some things you might observe in a child with ASD include the following:

- Communication:
  - ❯ not pointing or using other gestures
  - ❯ language developing slowly
  - ❯ difficulty in starting or maintaining conversation
  - ❯ reversing the pronouns "I" and "you"
  - ❯ repetition of memorized passages.
- Social interaction:
  - ❯ withdrawn
  - ❯ does not play interactively

> minimal eye contact

> difficulty making friends

> lack of empathy.

- Behavior:

  > very narrow, obsessive interests

  > aggressive or violent

  > strong need for routine

  > tantrums

  > repetitive body movements

  > little pretend play

  > unusual approaches to sensory stimulation.

The types of difficulties that any one child might have in these three areas can range widely (hence the use of the term "spectrum"). A child with autism may be verbal or nonverbal, aggressive or withdrawn, overly or inadequately sensitive to stimulation, a devoted gourmet or a finicky eater, up all night or able to sleep through the apocalypse. There is no common characteristic shared by all. It is the overall constellation of symptoms that leads to a diagnosis of ASD.

We wish to state very clearly the unpopular and unwelcome truth that **autism cannot be cured**. Any "miracle stories" you have heard about children being cured of autism are not true. Children whose autistic symptoms disappeared completely upon undertaking some treatment or intervention were not autistic to begin with, though they may have been misdiagnosed. It is also certainly true, though, that the symptoms of autism can be managed and often markedly reduced by various treatments and interventions.

WHY WE WROTE THIS BOOK

This is not a book that will make recommendations, nor will it promote or condemn certain treatments or interventions. Although we, the authors, are behavioral scientists and have opinions about the quality of evidence supporting various treatments and interventions, we have written this book to be informative, not judgmental. We understand that parents will make choices about interventions that are motivated by combinations of anxiety, hope, values, beliefs and practicality. Although the decisions that individual families will make about autism interventions are not always driven by scientific data, we nonetheless think it is critically important for parents not only to know the scientific data in a basic sense, but also to be aware of which interventions possess minimal supporting evidence. Lack of evidence need not be a contraindication for choosing an intervention, but parents need to understand the foundations of their decisions. **We want to reduce the number of interventions that are undertaken because of misunderstandings or misperceptions. Too many times, we have encountered families who have chosen interventions based upon information they believed to be true, but which was not.**

Books such as this one offer several advantages over searching or browsing the internet. It is easy to drown in internet information, as embedded links take searchers off in unforeseen directions. Without very careful, systematic tracking of the search process, the sources of information often become unclear. You may find yourself asking "Where did I find this information? Who recommended this? What was this person's expertise?" This is especially problematic when presented with contradictory information from different sources, a situation which requires remembering and reconstructing the information in a way that allows for reflective deliberation. While many people recognize that some internet content is not credible, it can be difficult to sort out the wheat from the chaff. Our book is intended to offer the comfort of expert credibility. We hope that it becomes a portable, reliable, working reference guide—one that you make notes in, discuss with others, take to doctors' appointments and school meetings, and share with other families.

What we know about ASD changes very rapidly. Does this mean that this book will be obsolete before sunset? No! The treatments we present in this book are not new in the truest sense of the word. Most have been used since at least the early 2000s and show no signs of declining in popularity. Treatment ideas that are freshly emerging, if they have merit, will take many years to become established, and many more years to be scientifically studied.

WHAT WE COVER IN THE BOOK, AND WHAT WE DON'T

Each of our 15 treatment chapters covers a different approach to treating children with ASD. This is by no means an exhaustive list; hundreds of potential therapeutic interventions have been embraced by families in their quests to manage ASD. The topics we have selected represent the most common, though sometimes controversial, interventions. Most are the therapies and treatments that will pop up in a typical internet search, and which appear frequently in books about autism and ASD. A few others are included because of their long and durable history. Because we wanted this book to be an essential guide to the basics, we have not reviewed treatments that have been largely left behind, forming the history of ASD interventions (e.g., rebirthing). Nor have we included treatments considered to be on the fringes of the field, though some of these treatments may in time attain status and respect as truly successful interventions. Finally, we are not claiming that treatments outside of this book have no potential value or purpose. We are simply confining ourselves to the core interventions most readily accessible to parents of children with ASD—bringing a body of useful information into ready reach.

2 SCIENCE AND SCIENTIFIC VOCABULARY

Elisabeth Hollister Sandberg
and Becky L. Spritz

SCIENCE REQUIRES DATA

One of the premises of this book is that empirical evidence is essential to the evaluation of a treatment or intervention. In order for a treatment to have empirical support, someone must have scientifically measured things that demonstrate that this approach works. This is what distinguishes science and empiricism from opinions, beliefs, theories or logic. It does not matter whether someone thinks, no matter how reasonably, that a treatment is effective; effectiveness needs to be shown through observable, measurable results. Blogs, Wikipedia and other websites make it look as if treatments have empirical support, when they may not. In each of the treatment chapters of this book, we describe both the empirical and the non-empirical information about each treatment in order to help parents recognize and weigh the sources of claims.

THE VOCABULARY

Although we have endeavored to keep the evaluations of scientific evidence as simple and clear as possible, there is some unavoidable terminology associated with the methods used to conduct research about therapies and interventions. Rather than explaining it repeatedly within the chapters, we have decided to define our terms here, where they can be easily referenced. We encourage you to use this chapter as a resource, both for the chapters that follow and for clarification of outside sources of information. Recognize that some of the terms take on a different meaning in a scientific context than they carry in everyday talk. We present the terms in alphabetical order, but some of the definitions require an understanding of other definitions. Practically speaking, this means you will may need to skim through this chapter more than once. When you run into a word in *italics* in the explanations below, that word is defined elsewhere in the list.

ASD: We have chosen to use the acronym ASD to make reference to autism spectrum disorder(s) and autism spectrum diagnosis or diagnoses. We use ASD to refer broadly to the entire autism spectrum and generally avoid making distinct classifications such as "severe autism," "PDD" (pervasive development disorder) or "Asperger's."

Blind/Double-blind: "Blind" means that the participants in the study (the children or their families) do not know what treatment they are receiving. "Double-blind" means that neither the participants nor the person conducting the study know who is getting which treatment. This is an extremely important tool in treatment studies because it equalizes the *placebo* effect across conditions (all patients have the same expectation that they could be receiving a real treatment). It also means that the doctors, researchers and parents cannot inadvertently influence the treatment outcome. For example, imagine a fictional treatment study about a medication for reducing silliness in children. A nurse is in charge of distributing the medications to families participating in the study. Some families will get the silliness-reducing pill, and others will get a sugar pill (a *placebo*). If the parents know they are giving their child a silliness-reducing pill, they may report their child's behavior to be less silly later in the day just because they expected a reduction in silliness. If the parents are blind to their treatment group (not knowing whether they got silliness-reducing pills or sugar pills), this assures the researcher that the results are not due to the expected effects of the intervention. In a double-blind study the nurse handing out pills to the families would also not know which families received the silliness-reducing pill or the sugar pill, so the nurse could not accidentally be more or less encouraging to the family about the potential effects of the pills.

Case study: A case study is a specific type of research design in which the experiences or progress of a single person are described in great detail. For example, a child may be given a special diet to follow. Frequent detailed notes about that child's behavior are then taken over a long period of time. These data about the child are called the "case." Case studies allow for the in-depth examination of the effects of a treatment but there is no power to generalize; we cannot say that another individual would have the same experiences or progress. Case studies are less advantageous than other research designs because they do not allow for *control* or *randomization*. Even though case studies have very little explanatory power, they are frequently cited as evidence for ASD treatments and interventions. The experiences of one child may be interesting, and may suggest paths for future research, but they are not evidence that can be used to make decisions about other children.

Conflict of interest: In science, a conflict of interest means that a researcher stands to gain (through fame or fortune) if results of a particular study are favorable. This happens when the creator of a program, device or drug is personally studying its effectiveness. When researchers have a conflict of interest, any results they report should be interpreted very carefully. Cases of scientific fraud in which researchers fabricate positive results are rare (though this has happened). The chances of subtle biases, however, are very real. Ideally, any positive result found by a researcher with a conflict of interest would be replicated by a group of independent, objective researchers.

Control: Researchers often discuss the importance of controlling variables. This means we hold constant certain characteristics of the people we are studying because we want to make sure that any differences we observe are due to the treatments and not to differences between the individuals in the treatment groups. For example, a group of twenty children participate in an intervention study to improve children's reading—ten of the children watch Program A, and ten watch Program B. At the end of the study, the results indicate that the children who watched Program A are better readers, but it turns out that the children who watched Program A were also older than those who watched Program B. One cannot discern if the results are due to the advantage of watching Program A, or if they are due to age (because older children are better readers). Interpreting the results of any study requires taking a careful look at which variables were controlled and which were not. Every uncontrolled variable represents a possible alternative explanation for the results.

Control group: In a treatment study, a control group consists of a group of people who participate in the study, but who do not receive the treatment. If you have ten five-year-olds participate in a special language program, you would want to compare their progress with ten other five-year-olds who did not participate in the language program. A control group allows you to compare the effects of a treatment to any changes in symptoms or behavior when no treatment is applied; it is the only way to be certain that such changes are not just due to natural factors, such as maturation. In the case where no treatment is given, this is called a no-treatment control group. A control group could also be given a *placebo* treatment to make the study even better!

Crossover study: A crossover study involves different groups of individuals receiving different treatments at different times and (sometimes) in different orders. This is similar to what you might do if you were informally testing if your child's rash might be attributable to your new laundry detergent. You use the detergent for a week, noting the status of the rash. You switch to a different detergent for a week and notice that the rash is gone. Does this mean the detergent was responsible? Not necessarily; perhaps the rash was from a virus that has run its course, or from some other chemical change. To be sure, you go back to using the old detergent for a week and watch for the rash. You switch to the new detergent again and watch. Having multiple data points enables you to say with some confidence whether the rash was or was not detergent related.

Homogeneity (homogeneous group): A homogeneous group is one in which all of the members are very similar (perhaps the same age, the same gender, the same level of diagnosis, the same race or ethnicity, the same level of family income). The Toy Story Martians represent an extremely homogeneous group of toys. Studying a homogeneous group makes us more confident that all of the participants could be expected to respond to the treatment in similar ways, but it also limits the generalizability of our results to individuals similar to the group being studied (i.e., generalizing from the Toy Story Martians to other types of toys). This is in contrast to a heterogeneous group, wherein the members are different. All of the Toy Story characters (Woody, Buzz, the Potato Heads, Slinky and the Martians) together form a heterogeneous group. Heterogeneity allows for greater generalization (to toys, in general), but is less *controlled*.

Meta-analysis: A meta-analysis is a systematic, mathematical *review* of the research literature using the actual data (the numbers) collected by many other researchers to conduct a more comprehensive statistical analysis. It is akin to an overall review of a movie, using all of the reviews from all of the available sources (every newspaper and magazine that has reviewed the movie)—though more scientific. A meta-analysis can be conducted only if sufficient statistical data have been collected on a particular treatment approach. A meta-analysis is, therefore, in and of itself, indicative that an intervention has been fairly well researched.

Placebo: A placebo is a substance or a procedure that has no known therapeutic effect (e.g., a sugar pill). A placebo effect occurs when something changes simply because one expected it to change. Good research studies will often use a placebo *control group*. This would be a group of participants who are receiving a "fake" treatment (or simply a treatment that is expected to have no effect) but do not know it. A relaxation therapy, for example, might be compared to yoga for treatment of anxiety. Participants in both groups are likely to believe that they are receiving a treatment and therefore expect to feel less anxious because they are receiving an intervention. If the relaxation therapy is truly effective for reducing anxiety, though, those who participate in it should demonstrate more improvement in functioning than the yoga group. Including a placebo group allows the researcher to compare the effects of a treatment to what people expect to happen when they receive a treatment, which is a more rigorous scientific comparison. Comparing a real treatment to a placebo allows a researcher to determine whether an intervention has an effect above and beyond an individual's expectations.

Prospective: By definition, prospective means planning something in advance. A prospective treatment study is one in which a group of individuals is identified and then studied over time. A decided advantage to prospective studies is that they allow researchers to measure change from before the intervention started to after the intervention occurred. Let's say that someone has hypothesized that playing videogames leads to more aggressive storytelling. A prospective study would assess an individual's storytelling language, then let them play videogames, and then measure their storytelling language again. By contrast, a *retrospective* study examines how people think they have changed, without having an objective measure from before the intervention occurred.

Randomization: Randomization is a specific research technique wherein every individual has an equal chance of being assigned to a group. This scientific definition of the word random stands in sharp contrast to the lay definition, which implies that something occurs by luck or happenstance. For instance, a friend announces a trip to Europe and you ask, "How did you decide where to go?" Your friend might respond, "It was totally random! My mother was planning a trip to Spain, and I decided to join her!" But in science, random means something much more precise than unplanned. In a randomized treatment study, each individual has an equal chance of being assigned to each treatment (or to a no-treatment group). Thus, if a person's destination for a European vacation were randomly determined, there would an equal chance of going to any of the countries in the European Union. Likewise, if a group of twenty children with ASD are going to participate in a study comparing two different treatment programs, the names of ten children will be drawn out of a hat (metaphorically speaking) and those children are assigned to Treatment A. The others are assigned to Treatment B. An example of a study design that is not randomized would be to assign the ten children with ASD in Ms. Jones' class to Treatment A, while the ten children with ASD in Mr. Smith's class receive Treatment B. Instances in which individuals volunteer for a specific treatment also violate conditions of randomization. Although random assignment to treatments or group is the ideal way to conduct a study, there are many practical realities of studying children with ASD that make the practice extremely difficult.

Retrospective: In a retrospective study, an individual is looking back or researchers are examining data after the fact. (This is in contrast to a *prospective* study, in which data collection is planned in advance—see definition above.) Imagine a group of individuals who have been participating in a time management workshop at the local library. After completing the workshop, the participants might be asked to evaluate their new time management skills. The disadvantage to retrospective studies is that no "before" data exist to which to compare the "after" data. Thus, with a retrospective study, one can determine a level of performance after a treatment, but cannot know whether that level of performance actually represents an improvement over a prior level. Retrospective studies also cannot be *randomized*. This increases the possibility that some unrecognized factor drives the observed results instead of the factor the researcher thought was causing the result.

Review: A review, more technically called a systematic review or comprehensive review, is when a researcher undertakes the extensive and laborious process of finding and analyzing all of the research work that has been done by other researchers on a given topic. For example, systematic review of the effects of a particular vitamin supplement would involve finding, summarizing and evaluating all of the published research about that supplement. This is similar to a *meta-analysis*, except that a review does not consolidate the numerical data of these different reports; instead, it gives overall impressions and summaries.

Sample: In science, a sample is the group of people being studied. We study samples because it is impossible to examine the effects of a treatment on every single person. When cooking a pot of chili, the chef is interested in knowing whether the level of seasoning is right (not too hot, just spicy enough!). To determine this, the chef does not taste every single bean in the pot, but instead chooses a spoonful of beans thought to represent the spiciness of the entire batch. Likewise, we use the results from a sample to draw conclusions about how a treatment might affect a larger population of individuals. In studies of children with ASD, we hope that the samples studied accurately represent the larger population of all individuals with ASD. Sometimes you will see references to "n," which refers to the size of the group or sample. For instance, if you studied five children, you would say that your sample size was five, or that n=5.

Significant: The term "significant" has a very specific meaning in science. A significant finding is one that has proven to be statistically very unlikely to have occurred by chance. You can think of a claim of a "significant difference" as being a scientific way of saying a "mathematically real" difference. Although saying that a difference is significant means that it is a mathematically proven difference, nothing is implied about the size of that difference. Imagine that agricultural scientists are studying whether adding a special growth hormone to corn fertilizer increases the crop yield. Let's say that they find that corn plants treated with the new fertilizer are statistically significantly larger than untreated plants. The crops have been mathematically proven to be different, but the difference in yield between the two crops is less than five grams! You can have mathematical significance without having practical (or clinical) significance. When scientists want to make claims about the size or impact of a difference they use words such as "substantial" instead, or move into more complicated math about "effect sizes."

What does all of the above terminology translate to when one is evaluating the quality of research? The very best conclusions about cause and effect (being able to say that an intervention causes a change) are achieved when you combine randomization with placebos, a control group and blindness. What you get is called a randomized double-blind placebo controlled experiment. This is the most credible and convincing tool that scientists have in their arsenals and allows us to draw firm conclusions about how well a treatment works. This is also, admittedly, very difficult to achieve due to the practical considerations of the cost, effort and organization required to do the experiment. Indeed, with respect to the treatments for ASD outlined in this book, there are few interventions that meet these rigorous standards.

WHY CAN'T WE HAVE SOLID EVIDENCE FOR EVERYTHING?

If the randomized double-blind placebo controlled experiment is the gold standard in scientific research, why isn't **all** autism treatment research conducted using this method? The reality of the situation is that researchers often cannot construct ideal research projects. We cannot put children with ASD in artificial environments; eliminate their educational, familial and social contexts; or feed them whatever we want. And, even though the incidence of ASD is higher now than it ever has been, there are still not many children with ASD in any one community or school who are available and willing to participate in research studies. Researchers try to make the best of studying the children they have available, under the circumstances in which they live. This means that some research studies are definitely of higher quality than others. Sometimes an accumulation of suboptimal studies can make a meaningful scientific contribution when they are considered collectively.

3 APPLIED BEHAVIORAL ANALYSIS

Mallory L. Dimler and
Elisabeth Hollister Sandberg

WHAT IS APPLIED BEHAVIORAL ANALYSIS?

Applied Behavioral Analysis (ABA) is a comprehensive,
behavioral treatment program designed to increase positive
skills and behaviors, and to decrease problematic behaviors
in children with ASD. ABA involves having trained
therapists make careful observations of specific behaviors
and the factors that trigger these behaviors. Positive
reinforcement is then used to shape behavior into new pro-
social skills. Problematic behaviors are addressed by not
providing reinforcement for them. ABA is implemented
in both structured (e.g., school-based ABA program) and
unstructured (e.g., at home) environments, so that the child
can learn how to generalize behavior changes across settings.

The term "Early Intensive Behavioral Intervention" (EIBI)
refers to programs of 25 or more hours per week of one-
on-one ABA therapy for very young children (ages two to
six). The term EIBI, for all intents and purposes, is the same
thing as "ABA program" when referring to interventions
with young children.

HOW DOES APPLIED BEHAVIORAL ANALYSIS SUPPOSEDLY WORK AS A TREATMENT FOR ASD?

The development of ABA was influenced by the Young Autism Project (YAP), a highly structured behavioral program for children with ASD created by O. Ivar Lovaas in 1970. This program was designed to provide individualized, one-to-one behavioral training in the child's home.

ABA is based on the principles of behaviorism, a psychological learning theory that explains how people learn and behave. Behaviorism asserts that an individual's actions are neither random nor unpredictable; all behaviors have a purpose. According to this theory, behaviors that are reinforced (for which a positive consequence occurs) are more likely to be repeated. Although this seems to be a straightforward idea, reinforcement can be a subtle and extremely complicated thing. Our tendency is to view reinforcement as a transparent positive event (such as receiving praise for doing something right). When looking at the behaviors of ASD the notion of reinforcement goes much deeper than simply receiving parental approval or disapproval in response to a behavior. If a child with ASD regularly engages in an undesirable behavior, that behavior is occurring because the consequences of the behavior are in some way rewarding for the child. The central goal of ABA is for the child with ASD to learn specific skills that will increase the likelihood of becoming as independent and successful as possible in the future—skills such as being able to greet people politely, request things, stand in line and button a coat.

The first step in initiating ABA therapy is for a licensed ABA therapist to conduct a Functional Behavioral Analysis. During a Functional Behavioral Analysis, positive and negative behavior patterns—patterns that promote or interfere with functioning within the family or classroom— are identified. Building on the principles of learning theory and behaviorism, the ABA therapist formulates theories about what triggers various behaviors and how those behaviors are reinforced. With input from parents and teachers, an individualized plan is developed to specifically address targeted behaviors. Specific intervention techniques (usually in the form of small and immediately gratifying rewards, which are called "positive reinforcers") are used to assist the child in producing and maintaining desired, socially meaningful behaviors. Problematic behaviors are purposely redirected or not reinforced (e.g., not responding to a child's screaming if it has been identified that the goal of screaming is to obtain a parent's attention). Continual monitoring and observation gives the therapist feedback regarding the child's progress so that treatment plans can be adjusted.

Within the field of ABA, there are two dominant intervention methods that are used to when treating ASD: discrete-trial teaching (DT) and pivotal response training (PRT).

Discrete-trial teaching

Discrete-trial teaching, also known as the Lovaas method, is what most people are referring to when they say "ABA." It is comprised of formal one-on-one training sessions between a child and an ABA therapist. Within each training session, one particular skill is practiced through repeated trials (attempts). The term "discrete" means that each trial is separate from the next. Trials are designed to be brief and are broken down into four parts: an instruction from the therapist, a response from the child, an immediate consequence for the response, and a short interval of down-time before starting the next trial.

Once the basic skills of a behavior have been mastered, complex skills (skills identified as important for the child to improve or increase) are broken down into smaller sets of basic subskills. Subskills are taught and reinforced through repeated trials of instruction, response and consequence, with trials repeated until a positive result is obtained consistently. For example, a family might decide that it is important for their four-year-old son with ASD to respond appropriately when greeted by another person. This is a complex skill. Subskills within this complex behavior include making eye contact, saying "Hi" back, and adding the name of the person. Initially the child will receive reinforcement for executing small parts of the desired response. Consider the following sample intervention:

Therapist Nancy is working with four-year-old Alex on responding appropriately to greetings. Nancy and Alex sit down facing each other (usually across a desk or table). Alex is not paying attention to Nancy. Nancy will brightly and loudly say, "Hi, Alex!" The tone of her voice will induce Alex to look at her. Nancy will immediately say, "Good looking!" while giving Alex a small reward (such as a pretzel or a raisin). There will be a brief period of inactivity (the interval) before Nancy repeats this exchange, which represents a behavioral sequence. When Alex learns that rewards are received for looking, he will be more likely to make eye contact when Nancy says, "Hi." Eventually Nancy will be able to reduce her tone to a more normal level.

Building on these skills, Nancy may then target getting consistent eye contact from Alex in response to her greeting. She models the desired behavior for him. When she says, "Hi, Alex!" Alex makes eye contact but says nothing while waiting for his treat. Nancy holds the treat up and says, "Say hi." She will repeat this until Alex at least makes the tiniest approximation of saying "Hi"—for which he will receive praise and his reward. Future trials will require making eye contact as well as saying "Hi" in order to earn a reward. By breaking down skills like this, behavior is shaped into the complete desired response.

Pivotal response training

Pivotal response training is a procedure that focuses on reinforcing and shaping pivotal behaviors that are essential for social, emotional and intellectual functioning. In contrast to DT, PRT is more loosely structured and uses naturally occurring teaching opportunities that spontaneously arise in the child's interactions with others. Strategies used in PRT include organizing the environment to include the child's preferred toys and activities that, through behavior initiated by the child, can be used to reinforce positive pivotal behaviors.

For example, nonverbal six-year-old Lindsay is playing in the toy area in her preschool. Lindsay reaches out for a block to add to her tower. Therapist Nancy holds the block back, looks at Lindsay and says, "Block." Lindsay says "Blah," and then is given the block as a reward for her verbal request. Over time, the requesting skill can be built up into clearly saying "Block," and eventually, "I want the block."

WHAT WILL YOU READ ON THE INTERNET ABOUT APPLIED BEHAVIORAL ANALYSIS AS A TREATMENT FOR ASD?

There are common, persistent myths about ABA on the internet. Some will refer to ABA as a "philosophy," implying that it reflects the basic belief systems of its proponents (in other words, they say that people who believe in ABA as an effective treatment must believe that children can be reduced to a collection of trained behaviors). ABA is not a philosophy, however: it is an evidence-based scientific technique that uses the methods of experimentation (e.g., careful observation, measurement, manipulation of environment) to identify factors responsible for behavioral change. Critics will also argue that ABA produces "robot children" who are trained to perform certain tasks on demand and who can execute those skills only in artificially constructed environments and situations. Advocates defend the skill acquisition process by saying that a skill that does not come naturally must be artificially learned and practiced before it can be generalized to more natural settings.

Be alert for the use of strong language in online discussions of ABA, many of which contain misrepresentations and inaccurate information. Some media sources claim that ABA can help a child "overcome ASD" or "lose an ASD diagnosis."[1] Although ABA effectively increases pro-social behaviors and decreases problematic behaviors for children with ASD, it does not cure autism. One will also read claims that ABA is "torture," will "traumatize your child," and "causes much harm." Although ABA requires diligent effort and may be challenging and stressful for both parents and children, scientific research indicates that ABA is not dangerous or harmful for children and that the procedures are safe. Notably, ABA no longer uses aversive consequences, or punishments, when children engage in problematic behaviors (e.g., slapping; shocking). Prior to the 1980s there were extreme programs that did employ aversive consequences, but any claims that ABA uses such techniques are inaccurate.

ABA therapists are either Board Certified Behavioral Analysts (BCBAs) or Board Certified Associate Behavior Analysts (BCABAs).[2] To become a BCBA, one must receive advanced formal training and at least a Master's degree, participate in supervised work designing and conducting ABA interventions, and pass the Behavior Analyst Certification Board examination. BCABAs have fewer qualifications, including undergraduate-level coursework in behavioral analysis, supervised work conducting ABA interventions, and passing the BCABA examination. BCABAs practice under the supervision of BCBAs. Other professionals may have completed training in ABA before the BCBA certification program was developed and still others have participated in training workshops (e.g., as a part of teacher development courses). The Autism Special Interest Group of the Association of Behavior Analysis International urges parents to ask for documented credentials when hiring an ABA therapist.[3]

The internet is inundated with anecdotal reports about the use of ABA for ASD. Many parents discuss the improvements their children have experienced as a result of ABA while other stories highlight the challenges that parents may experience with learning ABA and the stress associated with implementing it at home. Some parents report negative experiences with ABA therapists and programs that do not follow ABA procedures appropriately. Other parents report frustration because they know ABA is a scientifically supported treatment for ASD but they cannot access or afford ABA services. Parents seeking help on this issue frequently receive tips and suggestions from other parents, including advice for accessing ABA treatment.

WHAT DO SCIENTISTS SAY ABOUT APPLIED BEHAVIORAL ANALYSIS?

Although research supports ABA as being successful in improving core deficits in ASD, like any other treatment, it is not a cure. Some of the earliest high quality scientific support for ABA was Lovaas' 1987 Early Intervention Project.

Dr. O. Ivar Lovaas studied 38 children with ASD who were under four years old.[4] Half of the children participated in one-on-one intensive behavioral treatment, mostly discrete-trial training, for approximately 40 hours a week. The remaining children served as a control group, and received ten hours or fewer of the same one-on-one behavioral treatment. Children who participated in the intensive treatment for two or more years experienced significant improvements in IQ, social and school functioning. The inclusion of a control group and the use of a homogeneous sample of children gives strength to these conclusions.

Since then, additional research has pointed to the increased likelihood of achieving success with ABA if interventions are started at a young age (before the age of five years). One particular research team examined 34 studies that had been conducted on the effects of ABA programs for young children with ASD. Generally, children with ASD who participated in Early Intensive Behavioral Intervention across these studies experienced improvements in IQ, communication and social skills, and daily living skills. The evidence, though compelling, is not perfect. Only nine of the studies included a treatment group and a control group for comparison. Also, when comparing EIBI with any other intervention, one needs to establish that the effects are due to the behavioral intervention itself, and do not simply stem from spending 30 hours per week with a highly educated, attentive adult. Studies are needed in which EIBI is compared to other interventions conducted with similar intensiveness and by comparably trained adults.

Because of its behavioral focus, ABA is one of the most widely researched treatments for ASD. Moreover, the research on ABA is most consistent with the scientific standards for evaluating effective treatments (see Chapter 2 on Science and Scientific Vocabulary). In fact, in 2012, researchers reviewed the cumulative body of evidence on ABA through an examination of five different meta-analyses.[5] This collective evidence definitively indicates that early intensive ABA programs can be powerful interventions that produce large gains in IQ and adaptive behaviors among children with ASD.

In conclusion, ABA has been recognized as a primary, scientifically supported treatment for ASD by the US Surgeon General and the American Academy of Pediatrics.[6, 7] ABA treatment methods were also recognized in 2009 as "established treatments" for ASD by the National Autism Center's National Standards Project, indicating that there is sufficient compelling scientific evidence to conclude that ABA is an effective ASD intervention.[8] Currently researchers are working on designing ABA programs that balance a structured format and natural settings, to increase the likelihood of rapid skill attainment and generalization across settings.

WHAT ARE THE COSTS OF APPLIED BEHAVIORAL ANALYSIS?

ABA treatment programs are frequently school based, and thus free of charge to qualifying families. School funding and resources may vary, though, and systems are seldom able to provide a full-time (30–40 hours per week) ABA program. Private ABA therapy is extremely expensive. Cost estimates for a full-time private ABA program range from $30,000 to $50,000 a year. Because of the strong scientific support for the effectiveness of ABA as a treatment for ASD, insurance coverage for ABA services is improving, but blanket coverage is still not the norm.

Parental and familial involvement and skilled ABA therapists increase treatment effectiveness and generalization.

Parents can be taught to implement ABA teaching plans, but regular professional consultation with an ABA therapist is required—not only to conduct the Functional Behavioral Analysis but also to evaluate data and update teaching plans accordingly. Licensed ABA therapists usually charge at least $50 per hour, though this varies widely by region and level of experience. An ABA program requires a large time commitment and a great deal of consistent effort.

APPLIED BEHAVIORAL ANALYSIS (ABA)

Ages	→	most effective in young children		
Anecdotal parental support	→	not much	mixed	positive
Scientific evidence	→	weak	moderate	strong
Availability	→	limited	moderate	wide
Cost (time and money)	→	minimal	moderate	high

4 CHELATION

Jill Myerow Bloom and
Elisabeth Hollister Sandberg

WHAT IS CHELATION?

Chelation is a process for removing heavy metals from the human body when they reach toxic levels. These metals include lead, aluminum and mercury, the last of which has been implicated as a potential cause of ASD. The process involves using a chelator, a chemical that binds to heavy metals in the body so that they can be eliminated from the body through urination. Chelators can be administered intravenously, orally or transdermally.

HOW DOES CHELATION SUPPOSEDLY WORK AS A TREATMENT FOR ASD?

Chelation is a commonly used FDA-approved medical treatment for addressing metal poisoning.[1] When done properly under the supervision of a medical physician, chelation is a safe treatment for metal toxicity. The symptoms of lead poisoning, including abdominal pain, fatigue and learning problems, are successfully reduced as chelator-bound lead molecules are excreted from the body. In addition to removing lead, chelation can be used to remove other metals present in toxic levels in the body, including aluminum, cadmium and mercury. Chelation has also been used experimentally to treat a wide range of disorders, including ASD.

Chelation was first promoted as a treatment for autism in the mid-1980s when the idea that autism might be caused by mercury poisoning first arose. If one believes that mercury exposure causes ASD, then using chelation to treat ASD is a logical solution. As chelation removes toxic mercury from the body, a reduction in symptoms of ASD should follow. Proponents of this treatment suggest that chelation leads to significant improvements in ASD children's behavior including gains in speech, attention and listening, and reductions in self-stimulating behaviors.

Although oral chelators are available for purchase by non-physicians, it is strongly recommended that chelation treatment be prescribed and supervised by a trained physician. There is currently no standard regimen for physicians to follow for chelation for ASD. Chelation specialists suggest that chelation (for any reason) must continue until metals are no longer found in children's urine samples—a process that can take months to years, depending on the child. Chelation is not FDA approved for the treatment of ASD or any other neuro-developmental disorder.

WHAT WILL YOU READ ON THE INTERNET ABOUT CHELATION AS A TREATMENT FOR ASD?

The internet contains substantial information about chelation as a treatment for ASD. The controversy surrounding chelation treatment for ASD is extensive, and is readily apparent in the contradictory information available on the internet. Until very recently, search results were dominated by websites that presented chelation as a safe and effective treatment for ASD, which was regarded by many as a direct result of mercury poisoning.

There has been enormous controversy about the relationship between ASD and vaccines that contain mercury. It is critical to note that many of the very convincing claims about a link between mercury and ASD are based on personal opinion rather than scientific fact. There has been a strong movement in the popular literature attempting to demonstrate that exposure to mercury in general, and the mercury-based preservative Thimerosal (found in the measles-mumps-rubella (MMR) vaccination) in particular, causes ASD. This theory has received anecdotal support from parents of children with ASD. They report personal observations that their children developed normally until receiving the MMR vaccine, at which point, they started showing symptoms of ASD. Celebrities such as Jennie McCarthy and Robert F. Kennedy Jr. have publicly supported the claim that mercury exposure causes ASD.

It has been argued that individuals with ASD present with reduced ability to excrete toxic metals, which would suggest that individuals with ASD would have higher levels of mercury in their system than non-autistic people. However, this "mercury poisoning" hypothesis has not been supported in the research. There are multiple studies demonstrating equivalent levels of mercury in the bodies of children with and without ASD.[2, 3] The absence of elevated levels of mercury in children with ASD suggests that they would not benefit from chelation treatment. Thus, there is no logical and scientific support for using chelation to reduce ASD symptoms, as the presumed mercury poisoning in ASD has never been supported through scientific research.

More recently, the public information tide has changed in favor of the above information. The causes and treatments promoted by mercury hypothesis supporters are thought to be implausible and incorrect by mainstream medical researchers and others in the scientific community. Scientists caution against, and even condemn, using chelation as a treatment for ASD. Medical experts refute the use of chelation to treat ASD primarily on the basis that ASD is not caused by mercury exposure. They assert that Thimerosal in vaccines cannot be the cause of ASD for a number of reasons: first, when Thimerosal was used as a preservative in vaccines, the amount of mercury in the vaccines was very small and children with ASD did not show the typical signs of mercury poisoning; second, children with ASD did not have increased concentrations of mercury in their systems; and third, the incidence of ASD has not decreased since Thimerosal was removed from the MMR vaccine. The scientific community has repeatedly demonstrated that there is no link between mercury-containing vaccines and ASD incidence. As such, they strongly argue that it is irresponsible and dangerous to treat children with chelation in the absence of evidence implicating mercury in the etiology of ASD.

The popular press provides evidence of the significant risk associated with chelation, including news stories reporting the deaths of young children during chelation treatment. This portion of the literature questioning the safety and effectiveness of chelation treatment for ASD stands in stark contrast to chelation's vocal supporters. In considering this highly controversial treatment, it is very important to access valid and reliable sources of information. Unfortunately, the sources that parents are likely to encounter vary widely in their quality.

WHAT DO SCIENTISTS SAY ABOUT CHELATION?

The scientific community has devoted a huge amount of resources to testing the mercury hypothesis: the belief that ASD is caused by exposure to mercury through the MMR vaccine. One deeply flawed study from 1998 (which was later retracted by the publisher) suggested a possible link between mercury and ASD, but more current, methodologically sound research demonstrates no causal relationship. An extensive review of the epidemiological studies examining the mercury hypothesis was conducted by the Institute of Medicine in 2004.[4] This report concluded that mercury exposure is not involved in the etiology of ASD and that vaccines are safe. Other review articles have replicated these findings.[5, 6, 7] These studies suggest that the relationship between vaccines and the onset of ASD is coincidental and temporal; ASD symptoms tend to emerge around the same age that the MMR vaccine is given (approximately 18–24 months), causing parents to conclude that the vaccine caused the symptoms. The failure to demonstrate a causal link between mercury-containing vaccines and ASD suggests that chelation is not an appropriate treatment for ASD.

To date, one randomized controlled trial has been conducted to actually assess the effects of chelation on symptoms of ASD.[8] In this study, the sociability, expressive and receptive language, and overall ASD severity of children with ASD who received multiple rounds of chelation were compared with children who received a single round of chelation plus six rounds of placebo treatment. Results of this study found that both groups demonstrated significant improvements across all symptom domains. Symptom improvements were just as good for the comparison group (who received one round of chelation) as for the experimental group (who received multiple rounds of chelation).

Note that this study did not include a placebo group (children who did not receive any chelation). Thus, this study demonstrates that multiple rounds of chelation have no added benefit over a single treatment. However, in order to conclude that chelation causes reductions in ASD symptoms, research would need to demonstrate that chelation is associated with more improvement than no chelation treatment at all. To date, no studies have addressed this issue. Interestingly, two planned National Institute of Mental Health (NIMH) studies examining the effect of chelation on ASD symptomatology have been cancelled. The NIMH has reportedly cancelled the studies due to dangers associated with chelation as well as a lack of scientific evidence to support the mercury hypothesis. Given this, reliable scientific evidence supporting the use of chelation to treat ASD is not likely to be forthcoming.[9]

Finally, the scientific evidence suggests that there is significant danger associated with treating ASD with chelation. Potential permanent side effects of chelation are well documented. They include kidney damage, liver damage, bone marrow damage and irregular heartbeats. Chelation treatment has been linked with death from cardiac arrest. At least 30 deaths from the side effects of chelation have been reported.[9] These deaths all occurred in medical facilities under the supervision of trained professionals, thereby demonstrating the significant risk associated with this process. Given the dangers associated with chelation and the lack of empirical evidence to support its use, the sum total of the scientific literature suggests that chelation is neither a safe, theoretically sound, nor effective treatment for ASD. Parents who nonetheless elect to use chelation as an ASD treatment should not chelate their children independently of knowledgeable physicians.

WHAT ARE THE COSTS OF CHELATION?

Insurance companies do not cover the costs of chelation to treat ASD because chelation is not an approved medical treatment for ASD. Hence, the costs associated with treating ASD using chelation can be substantial. Chelation sessions, which can last two to four hours, typically cost between $75 and $150 each. The number of sessions recommended by practitioners varies from five to more than 40. Overall estimates place the cost of chelation therapy for ASD at approximately $3000 to $4000. In addition to the price of chelation sessions, numerous medical tests should be completed throughout treatment to monitor metal excretion, metal content in the child's system and relevant other indicators. Finally, and most importantly, the medical risks associated with chelation are significant. For this reason, if not prescribed by a doctor, chelators are difficult but not impossible to obtain. Chelators are available from online retailers; however, many of them are approved to ship only to addresses outside of the United States. On average, these oral chelators cost approximately $45 dollars for a two- to six-month supply.

CHELATION			
Ages	→	any age	
Anecdotal parental support	→	not much	mixed	positive
Scientific evidence	→	weak	moderate	strong
Availability	→	limited	moderate	wide
Cost (time and money)	→	minimal	moderate	high

5
CRANIOSACRAL THERAPY

Nicholas D. Taylor and
Elisabeth Hollister Sandberg

WHAT IS CRANIOSACRAL THERAPY?

Craniosacral Therapy (CST) is a non-invasive treatment most commonly offered by chiropractors, osteopaths, occupational therapists and massage therapists. Therapists and practitioners use the method to treat a wide variety of disorders, ranging from migraines to ASD. According to practitioners of CST, disease and poor health can be attributed to disruptions in the rhythmic flow of the fluid surrounding the brain and spinal cord. Therapists use their hands to detect these disruptions, which they believe are caused by blockages and restrictions in the craniosacral system. Therapists then apply light, rhythmic pressure to the bones of the skull and sacrum (the triangular bone in the center of the lower back) to re-establish the rhythm, optimizing the flow of fluid around the brain and spine, reducing symptoms.

HOW DOES CRANIOSACRAL THERAPY SUPPOSEDLY WORK AS A TREATMENT FOR ASD?

CST is based primarily on the work of William Sutherland in the early 1900s. Sutherland believed that the bones of the skull are flexibly structured to allow for cyclical brain movements similar to respiration. He described a system in which the cranial bones shift in response to tension changes in dural membranes, the protective sheaths covering the brain and spinal cord. Cerebral-spinal fluid within the membranes flows rhythmically up and down the spinal column in a "craniosacral rhythm." As this rhythm occurs, the surrounding bones and membranes adjust in response to these shifts in pressure, else the craniosacral rhythm will be disrupted.[1]

According to this theory, any interruption of the craniosacral rhythm has the potential to degrade the functioning of the central nervous system and other body parts or systems, leading to dysfunction. Additionally, blockages in other parts of the body due to stress, trauma and injury can impact the craniosacral system. Thus, tissue restrictions anywhere in the body can affect the membranes surrounding the brain.

CST proponents propose that ASD is caused by a loss of flexibility in the membrane layers surrounding the brain. ASD is treated by enhancing the balanced motion of the dural membranes and the fluids moving into and out of the cranium. Practitioners of CST claim they can sense craniosacral rhythms throughout the body using their hands. Treatment is targeted at re-establishing one's natural craniosacral rhythm to alleviate symptoms and disease by "releasing" blockages in various parts of the body using light touch or massage.[1, 2]

Providers of CST are usually licensed osteopaths, chiropractors, naturopaths or massage therapists who offer the service in addition to their primary treatment modalities. However, there is no professional standard for training in CST and its practice is currently unregulated.

A typical session of CST lasts for an hour. The patient lies on a massage table while the therapist places his or her hands or fingers on specific areas of the body, attempting to sense areas of the body and skull in which the craniosacral rhythm is weak or strong. When CS therapists believe they have identified a blockage, they use techniques to unblock the area and re-establish the craniosacral rhythm. This is done by lightly pumping and pushing target areas on the skull, sacrum and other body tissues to increase flexibility and motion in these areas, and thereby allowing the body's natural craniosacral rhythm to occur unimpeded. Proponents suggest this can result in a range of outcomes, from subtle alleviation of ASD symptoms to significant improvement in overall functioning.[2]

WHAT WILL YOU READ ON THE INTERNET ABOUT CRANIOSACRAL THERAPY AS A TREATMENT FOR ASD?

The popular sources of information about treatments for ASD occasionally mention craniosacral and related osteopathic therapies and take different stances. For instance, the Association for Science in Autism Treatment discourages CST as a treatment for ASD because the treatment is "implausible" and lacks supporting research.[3] In contrast, the Autism-World website (known for promoting a wide variety of both conventional and unconventional treatments for ASD) offers an article promoting CST as a promising, useful treatment based on anecdotal parent reports.[4] The most readily available information about CST, though not specific to ASD, can be found on craniosacral, chiropractic or massage therapy websites created by practitioners or their member organizations. These websites usually provide a brief description of CST, a list of benefits, a history of the treatment, patient testimonials, links to other websites and a list of disorders for which it is claimed to be effective.

The Upledger Institute, founded by the originator of CST in 1985, offers a worldwide practitioner referral service with over 90,000 members, many training programs and a number of testimonials affirming its effectiveness as a treatment for problems including ASD. They primarily advocate for its use in conjunction with other interventions such as homeopathy and speech and language therapy.[1]

The numerous news articles, blog posts, digital videos, complementary medicine websites, ASD organization websites and skeptical websites that discuss CST vary widely in quality and content and frequently present information without making reference to their sources. CST is also often referred to as an "alternative" medical treatment because it is not accepted as a valid, mainstream treatment for any disorder, including ASD. CST remains an alternative treatment because it is based on a model of disease that conflicts significantly with science-based models of anatomy and physiology. Empirically based articles on CST, such as those on the Science-Based Medicine Blog, or the website Evidence-Based Medicine First, present skeptical articles about CST. These articles counter the theory behind craniosacral rhythms and reinforce mainstream medical understanding of anatomy and disease. Very few of these articles discuss the merits of CST as a treatment for ASD.

Overall, despite practitioners' consistent claims that it is an effective treatment, parents interested in CST will find it difficult to find explicit detailed evidence that CST is a beneficial intervention.

WHAT DO SCIENTISTS SAY ABOUT CRANIOSACRAL THERAPY?

Currently, there are no empirical studies examining the use of CST or its related therapies for treating symptoms of ASD. There is, however, a systematic review of 33 research studies directly examining different aspects of the CST model and its clinical applications.[2] This review concluded that existing studies of CST are low quality and do not provide support for CST's effectiveness as a treatment. A number of case studies, which give detailed accounts of single clients' treatment and progress, were also reviewed. Despite both positive and negative accounts of treatment effectiveness within the case studies, the unreliable nature of case studies and inconsistent results limit our ability to draw any conclusions about CST.

Highly relevant is a set of studies evaluating the ability of CS therapists to reliably detect the craniosacral rhythm. These studies look at inter-rater reliability—whether two therapists rating the same event produce the same results. In a CST study, this refers to the level of agreement between therapists who are assessing the CS rhythm. The five most recent studies have all found very low inter-rater reliability between assessors. For instance, a study conducted in 1994 had three CS therapists independently examine 12 children to determine their craniosacral rhythm rates. The ratings the therapists gave were unreliable, meaning that the rhythm rate given by one therapist for a child was different from the other therapists' assessments. This means that even under highly controlled conditions, it is unlikely that two CS therapists examining the same individual will report a similar CST rhythm. The fact that this result appears across studies suggests that the craniosacral rhythm is either nonexistent or, if it does exist, cannot be accurately measured—even by trained CS therapists.[2, 5]

These are highly problematic findings for CST, as the entire therapy is based on its practitioners being able to accurately identify the craniosacral rhythm in the body. Without the ability to detect CS rhythms, a CST practitioner cannot accurately claim that individuals with ASD have impaired CST rhythms, or that their treatment affects those CST rhythms. The findings are so problematic that they have led some osteopaths to call for the removal of craniosacral content from osteopathy school curriculums and licensing requirements. They argue that the inclusion of CST in the osteopathy curriculum, given the above findings, is harmful to the public, inconsistent with the goals of their field, and pseudo-scientific.

CST claims also fail to hold up with accepted, mainstream medical research. The first claim, that the brain and spinal cord are capable of making their own movements producing the craniosacral rhythm, is rendered implausible because the cells in these organs lack the microstructure necessary for movement. Scientific research also demonstrates that the bones in the skull relevant to CST undergo complete fusion between the ages of 12 and 19, such that they cannot be manipulated through light pressure.[5]

There is essentially no scientific evidence that validates CST as an effective treatment that can be reliably administered. Many aspects of the treatment and theory are incompatible with the established, peer-reviewed scientific literature. Currently, no high quality studies exist evaluating the effectiveness of CST as a treatment for any disorder, ASD included. Further, there is no empirical support for the craniosacral assumptions behind CST. Although the National Autism Center's National Standards Project reports Massage/Touch Therapy as an "emerging treatment" for ASD, the studies reviewed do not include CST.[6]

WHAT ARE THE COSTS OF CRANIOSACRAL THERAPY?

Monetary costs associated with CST range from $40 to $120 per hour, depending on the practitioner and area of the country. The number of sessions recommended by practitioners varies widely. All practitioners stress that treatment plans are highly individualized. Some refer to progress being made with just one treatment session, while others suggest three or more sessions per week for several weeks. One practitioner advises weekly sessions until the child is fully grown. Insurance does not cover the practice of CST. The Upledger Institute offers intensive therapy programs that run for five full consecutive days. The cost of these intensive programs is $3200.

CRANIOSACRAL THERAPY (CST)			
Ages	→	any age	
Anecdotal parental support	→	not much	mixed	positive
Scientific evidence	→	weak	moderate	strong
Availability	→	limited	moderate	wide
Cost (time and money)	→	minimal	moderate	high

6

DAILY LIFE THERAPY

Katherine K. Bedard and
Elisabeth Hollister Sandberg

WHAT IS DAILY LIFE THERAPY?

Daily Life Therapy (DLT) is an educational approach to treating children with ASD. Introduced to the United States in 1987, DLT is a school-based program that provides a broad and balanced educational curriculum incorporating academics, art, music, physical education, computer technology and social education. This treatment approach provides a highly consistent, highly structured environment for children with ASD and utilizes group dynamics and close bonds with teachers to develop understanding and trust. DLT is believed to improve emotional stability, concentration and awareness of surroundings without the use of any medications to control the symptoms of ASD.

HOW DOES DAILY LIFE THERAPY SUPPOSEDLY WORK AS A TREATMENT FOR ASD?

Dr. Kiyo Kitahara developed DLT in Tokyo, Japan in 1964 based upon her experiences teaching a child with ASD in a mainstream education kindergarten class.[1] DLT is grounded in the belief that education provides a path to find a child's individual identity and to help children to meet their full potential. DLT education is based on three interrelated principles that are integrated into every aspect of the school environment: vigorous physical exercise, emotional stability and intellectual stimulation. Through physical exercise children learn to regulate their own bodies. Exercise is also believed to promote health, stamina, mood stability, awareness of one's surroundings and concentration. Within this environment of exercise and consistent structure, teachers bond intimately with each student and help him or her to achieve emotional stability. This also provides the teacher with access to the child's potential intellectual development.

DLT is not just a set of techniques used to reduce the symptoms of ASD, but rather is a holistic, integrated approach to developing and educating the entire child—mind, body and spirit—through consistent reinforcement and practice within the classroom. The ultimate goal of DLT is lifelong inclusion in the community and a high quality of life. In a DLT school, children are placed in classrooms with small staff-to-student ratios, giving teachers the ability to address each child's specific needs. A typical day includes a curriculum focused on movement, music, art, physical exercise, group activities, imitation of the teachers, routine activities and vocational training. Behavior management in DLT never includes aversive measures, punishment, time-out procedures or medication. Emphasis is placed upon developing and maintaining a mutually trusting relationship between student and teacher that is based on love and understanding.

DLT in its purest form is available at only two schools: the Musashino Higashi Gakuen School in Tokyo, Japan, and the Boston Higashi School in Randolph, MA. The Rugeley Horizon School in Staffordshire, United Kingdom, established in 2000, utilizes an approach based on the principles of DLT. There is no formal training available for professionals outside of these schools to learn to practice DLT and implement the philosophy in other educational settings. Each of the schools that practice DLT offers slightly different day and residential programs for children diagnosed with ASD. The Musashino Higashi Gakuen School serves children in kindergarten to high school through a mixed education model.[2] Students with ASD are integrated with typical students for part of their day, and spend the rest of their time participating in the DLT curriculum. The Boston Higashi School currently serves more than 100 children between the ages of three and 22—all of whom have ASD.[3] The Rugeley Horizon School follows the general principles of DLT and is the most broad in its eligibility, welcoming students ages 4–19 with challenging behaviors and learning disabilities in addition to students diagnosed with ASD.[4]

Medications commonly used to manage the behavioral symptoms of ASD are not permitted in DLT programs. Dr. Kitahara, the founder of DLT, believed that medication is incompatible with DLT because it interferes with the child's ability to learn to regulate his or her own body. The side effects of medication are thought to interfere with children's natural ability to successfully learn and decrease their motivation to explore new things. By using the three core principles of DLT, children learn to naturally focus their attention, diffuse their energy, and feel calm and relaxed, allowing them to learn without the need for medication.

All children at the Boston Higashi School are provided with instruction consistent with the Massachusetts Curriculum Frameworks and must participate in the state's standardized testing process. Most teachers at the Boston Higashi School have at least a Master's degree in special education and are certified by the Massachusetts Department of Education.³ Information about formal approval or licensure for the Musashino Higashi Gakuen School is not widely available. The Rugeley Horizon School is accredited by the National Association of Independent Schools and Non-Maintained Special Schools (NASS). All students have access to the national curriculum, but the curriculum is individualized to meet each child's developmental needs.

WHAT WILL YOU READ ON THE INTERNET ABOUT DAILY LIFE THERAPY AS A TREATMENT FOR ASD?

Internet websites broadly dedicated to ASD generally include some information regarding the DLT approach (e.g., Autism Wiki, Raising Children Network, news articles, National Autistic Society, Research Autism). The most readily accessible internet information on DLT is published by the Boston Higashi School. The internet websites for all three schools provide numerous descriptive profiles of the experiences of individual students, as well as links to media articles and YouTube videos that paint pictures of success and support from parents and teachers. Parental endorsements on the websites indicate that most parents recognize that DLT does not cure ASD, but believe that it provides other important benefits such as improved coping skills, increased flexibility and improved appropriate functioning within the home community and family events.

Coverage of DLT on the internet is rather light compared with other treatments for ASD, probably because of the highly restricted accessibility to the treatment. There appears to be little controversy about the methods or the outcomes. Bear in mind, though, that very few families participate in the programs and those who do are highly invested in the success of the curriculum.

WHAT DO SCIENTISTS SAY ABOUT DAILY LIFE THERAPY?

To date, only one scientific research study on the effectiveness of DLT has been published.[5] When the Boston Higashi School first opened, six students diagnosed with ASD of similar age and behavioral patterns were chosen for intensive, systematic observation. All children were nonverbal and labeled as "low functioning" by parents and staff.

Weekly behavioral observations were conducted over a six-week period and again at a one-year follow-up. The study focused on three aspects of children's behavior: attending behavior (watching the teachers, task and/or other students), inappropriate responses (not being on task, not giving a desired response, making inappropriate vocalizations or actions) and appropriate responses (suitable situational responses required of students). Classroom teachers were not aware of which children were being observed—a factor that ensured the teachers would not treat the children being studied differently from the other children.

The results of the study indicated that children's attending behavior increased and inappropriate responses decreased between the initial observation period to the follow-up. Changes in measures of the children's appropriate responses were variable, and not consistently positive. Of the six students initially observed, three were no longer enrolled in the school at follow-up, and were not included in the study. The study's findings are therefore based upon an extremely small sample size, limiting generalizability. Moreover, because there was no comparison group, it is also possible that the changes observed over the two-year period could be attributed simply to maturation of the students. Consequently, there is no scientific evidence as yet to support the effectiveness of DLT as a treatment for ASD.

WHAT ARE THE COSTS OF
DAILY LIFE THERAPY?

The cost of a DLT school depends on whether the child attends the day or residential program. The Rugeley Horizon School website lists the cost to attend their day program at $130,000 annually, or $250,000 to $410,000 for children who board. According to a 2013 Massachusetts Special Education report of in-state program costs, the 2013 tuition for Boston Higashi School is $69,183 for day placement and $169,398 for residential placement.[6] In most cases, fees are covered by the child's public school district. The costs for the Musashino Higashi Gakuen School were not advertised. Once admitted, it is likely that families will be highly encouraged to continue enrolling their children for several years.

Non-monetary costs include the potentially taxing expectation of a close partnership and collaboration between the school and the parents. Parents are expected to maintain the philosophy and structure of the school environment within the home during evenings, weekends and school vacations. Additionally, some families may see the elimination of symptom-managing medications as a significant cost.

DAILY LIFE THERAPY (DLT)			
Ages →	school-age children		
Anecdotal parental support →	not much	mixed	positive
Scientific evidence →	weak	moderate	strong
Availability →	limited	moderate	wide
Cost (time and money) →	minimal	moderate	high

7

DEVELOPMENTAL INDIVIDUAL-DIFFERENCE RELATIONSHIP-BASED MODEL/FLOORTIME

Kristen L. Batejan and
Becky L. Spritz

WHAT IS DEVELOPMENTAL INDIVIDUAL-DIFFERENCE RELATIONSHIP-BASED MODEL/FLOORTIME?

The Developmental Individual-Difference Relationship-based (DIR) Model was developed as an intervention for children with ASD in the 1980s by Dr. Stanley Greenspan.[1] The DIR Model is best understood as a comprehensive framework designed to help parents, clinicians or teachers construct and tailor a treatment program based on the child's individual strengths and challenges. The DIR Model utilizes a team approach with collaboration between speech therapists, occupational therapists, teachers, parents and medical professionals. When people discuss DIR, they are most commonly referring to a specific therapeutic technique called Floortime, so named because the activities central to the therapy often occur via playing with young children on the floor. In Floortime, children's natural interests and play preferences are used to create challenges that will lead to social, emotional and intellectual growth. A core component of Floortime is building and sustaining emotional relationships with the child, making the one-on-one involvement of parents and other caregivers critical to treatment implementation.[2]

HOW DOES DIR/FLOORTIME SUPPOSEDLY WORK AS A TREATMENT FOR ASD?

DIR is based upon an extensive theoretical and conceptual orientation grounded in developmental psychology.[2] The DIR Model contains three key theoretical components:

- The **D** represents "developmental" and highlights the importance of tailoring the treatment of ASD to the developmental stage of the child.

- The **I** in DIR represents the need to tailor treatment to a child's individual differences, particularly individual differences in sensory motor processing and regulation. Knowing how a child regulates and responds to different sounds, touches and sights, and if a child is more or less sensitive to sensory input than most children, is critical to treatment.

- The **R** represents the relationship-based focus of the model. DIR helps children to build relationships with caregivers and others to develop emotional, social and cognitive capacities and skills. An assessment of the child's emotional development is used to individualize the child's treatment plan in accordance with his or her needs.

DIR is designed to facilitate children's social, emotional and intellectual growth surrounding six developmental stages and their corresponding milestones. Although typical children usually spontaneously acquire these developmental milestones by the age of four or five years, these milestones are often delayed in children with ASD. In DIR, the therapy involves developmentally appropriate, child-focused activities designed to help the child "climb" to higher developmental stages. Children with more severe symptoms of ASD are expected to progress more slowly through the stages compared with children with higher levels of functioning. The six developmental stages and corresponding therapeutic goals are as follows:

- **Self-regulation and shared attention:** in this stage the therapist helps the child learn to remain calm and to focus on his or her surroundings.

- **Engagement and relating:** the therapist encourages intimacy by modeling smiling, vocalizing, reaching and so forth. These behaviors help the caregiver to create an intimacy with the child where feelings can be incorporated into the relationship.

- **Two-way intentional communication:** back-and-forth interactions between the therapist and the child are built through child-led circles; for example, the child initiates a behavior (looks at a toy), the parent or adult follows the child's lead (picking up the toy) and then the circle is closed when the child acknowledges the parent (by taking the toy or smiling).

- **Purposeful, complex, problem-solving communication:** building on the simple two-way interactions of the previous stage, the therapeutic goal of this stage is for the child to communicate problem-solving needs.

- **Creating and elaborating symbols:** by using symbols and pretend play, the therapeutic goal is to move the child beyond communicating wants or needs to communicating about ideas.

- **Building bridges between symbols:** at this level, a high level of communication and interaction is required to build bridges between ideas. Therapeutic activities include seeking the child's opinion, debating with the child and negotiating with the child.

Within DIR, Floortime is a specific therapeutic technique involving play-based, developmentally appropriate activities. A distinguishing feature of Floortime is that it allows the child to take the lead in the interaction, all the while still working toward the designated developmental milestones and therapeutic goals. If, for instance, the therapeutic goal is to promote two-way intentional communication, the therapist may sit on the floor with the child with toys selected based upon the child's interests. Rather than present the child with a task (such as a book), and ask the child to name pictures in the book ("What is that? That is a kitten. Say kitten"), the therapist would wait for the child to initiate an activity (the child points to a kitten and says, "Ooh!") and then respond to the child in turn, modeling and shaping the child's behavior through positive interactions ("Oh, a kitten." The therapist crawls around on the floor and meows. "I'm a kitten!" The child responds and says, "Me, too!" And they laugh and return to the book for more). Each Floortime treatment plan looks different depending on the developmental stage of the child, the child's interests and the child's rate of development.

WHAT WILL YOU READ ON THE INTERNET ABOUT DIR/FLOORTIME AS A TREATMENT FOR ASD?

Floortime is often described as a play-based therapy that is used as a part of a larger, multi-treatment plan. Using Floortime techniques does not preclude using other therapeutic approaches. There is little online controversy and a general positive consensus about Floortime as a therapeutic intervention. Generally, parents seem to be quite pleased with the improvements emerging from the frequent and meaningful interactions that occur between parents and children during the treatment implementation. Satisfaction with the approach also stems from the fact that parents find the idea of individualized, developmentally appropriate, relationship building easy to understand and therefore easy to implement.

Floortime is less rigid than other behavioral interventions because there is no strict protocol that the family must follow. By its very nature, DIR/Floortime is conducive to individualization, and treatment plans can be easily changed depending on the improvements (or deteriorations) noted for any particular child. The Floortime experiences described online reveal a huge degree of variability in the structure, activities, time commitments and results.

Although there are some online forums through which parents can share ideas, strategies and successes, less testimonial evidence appears online for Floortime than for many other ASD treatments. Most of the online information is descriptive and informational. Claims of "cure" are rare and heated debate is essentially nonexistent.

WHAT DO SCIENTISTS SAY ABOUT DIR/FLOORTIME?

Although anecdotal reports from parents suggest that Floortime may be an effective intervention for ASD, the scientific evidence is lacking. Data-driven conclusions about Floortime are elusive because of the highly varied treatment approaches and because Floortime is seldom used as an exclusive therapeutic approach (and is instead a part of a combination of therapies). Without the ability to isolate a consistent treatment plan as the cause of a positive change, firm scientific conclusions about the effectiveness of Floortime cannot be drawn.

The published evidence for the effectiveness of Floortime as a treatment for ASD is limited to individual case studies and a single long-term follow-up study conducted by the originator of the technique.[1, 3, 4] Based upon the findings of this study, the researchers assert that Floortime can lead to improved emotional functioning, healthy peer relationships and increased intellectual abilities. It is important to note, however, that the researchers' affiliations with the technique represent a conflict of interest that could call into question the objectivity of the study.

The National Autism Center's National Standards Project places Floortime together with other developmental relationship-based treatments and classified this category in 2009 as "emerging treatments" for ASD.[5] Favorable outcomes have been documented, but additional high quality studies need to be conducted before we can say with confidence that they are indeed effective.

WHAT ARE THE COSTS OF DIR/FLOORTIME?

Floortime can be administered to children by therapists, teachers and parents. Families undertaking Floortime themselves need to hire a professional trained in Floortime to help create a personal and comprehensive program following the DIR Model. Qualified therapists charge $90–200 per hour depending on geographic location. Usually several hours are required for initial observations and planning.[6] Some parents choose to attend the workshops, training programs and conferences offered by Dr. Greenspan's organization (the Interdisciplinary Council on Developmental and Learning Disorders—the ICDL) or by certified therapists. Prices range depending on the professional's certification, but workshops seem to typically cost about $250, and full training programs run from $1000 to $3000.[2]

Floortime is often incorporated into special education curricula and thus may be provided free of charge to qualifying young children through the schools. Floortime is not a short-term therapeutic process. Intensive Floortime therapy is conducted for two to five hours per day over the course of several years. This type of intervention requires dedicated parents or family members to take the time to implement the DIR Model and Floortime.

A Brief Guide to Autism Treatments

DIR/FLOORTIME			
Ages	➤	most effective in young children	
Anecdotal parental support	➤	not much	mixed	positive
Scientific evidence	➤	weak	moderate	strong
Availability	➤	limited	moderate	wide
Cost (time and money)	➤	minimal	moderate	high

8 DIETARY SUPPLEMENTS

Elisabeth Hollister Sandberg
and Kristen L. Batejan

WHAT ARE DIETARY SUPPLEMENTS?

Dietary or nutritional supplements are ingestible non-food substances that contain vitamins, minerals and elements, enzymes, probiotics, anti-fungals, anti-bacterials, anti-virals, fiber, fatty acids or amino acids. They come in the form of pills, capsules, powders and liquids. Proponents claim that dietary supplements can be used to address nutritional deficiencies that cause ASD symptoms. Dietary supplements have been used to treat the symptoms of ASD since the 1960s, but the popularity of dietary supplements as an ASD intervention increased tremendously during the 1990s. The FDA does not regulate or approve supplements for the treatment of any condition.

HOW DO DIETARY SUPPLEMENTS SUPPOSEDLY WORK AS A TREATMENT FOR ASD?

Children with ASD are often finicky eaters. Restricted diets do not always allow for adequate, balanced nutrition. Also, there is evidence that children with ASD are more likely to have gastrointestinal disorders that may result in poor digestion and inadequate absorption of nutrients.[1] Dietary supplements are believed to treat symptoms of children with ASD via two possible mechanisms—by addressing nutritional deficiencies and by relieving gastrointestinal distress.[2]

A huge range of possible nutritional deficiencies has been linked, usually anecdotally, with ASD symptoms. Some of the supplements most commonly used as therapy for ASD include the following:

- **Melatonin:** melatonin as a supplement is a synthetic version of a hormone that is naturally produced by the body. Melatonin regulates sleep cycles.

- **Vitamin B6 and magnesium:** the B vitamins promote healthy nerve function and muscle tone. When combined with magnesium, vitamin B6 is claimed to improve eye contact, improvised speech and calmer behavior. Deficiencies in magnesium can lead to irritability, fatigue and poor coordination. Foods that are especially high in vitamin B6 include fish, meats, potatoes, nuts and bananas. Magnesium-rich foods include leafy green vegetables, seeds and legumes (e.g., pumpkin seeds, peanuts, black beans).

- **Essential fatty acids:** omega-3 fatty acids are essential for normal brain development. Fatty acids are thought to improve learning and behavior by stabilizing neurotransmitter levels in the brain. Fish, seeds and nuts are all good natural sources of fatty acids.

- **Vitamin C:** vitamin C is important for healing and for the production of neurotransmitters. It also acts as an antioxidant, protecting brain cells from oxidative stress. Vitamin C is found in fresh fruits and vegetables (citrus, cantaloupes, papayas, strawberries, bell peppers, kale, brussel sprouts). Vitamin C is not heat stable—the nutrient is destroyed during cooking.

- **Probiotics and digestive enzymes:** probiotics are said to improve digestive functions, which in turn may result in a reduction of aggressive ASD behaviors when abdominal discomfort is relieved. Biotics are friendly bacteria that live in our intestines and are essential for promoting digestion. Yogurt, cheese and other fermented food products contain these desirable bacteria. Probiotics are killed by heat.

- **DMG (dimethylglycine):** DMG (also called vitamin B15) is hypothesized to improve language and social functions by boosting circulation and nutrient absorption. Food sources for vitamin B15 include certain seeds (e.g., sunflower, sesame and pumpkin seeds), meats and brown rice.

Theoretically, by determining which deficiencies a child with ASD has, a regimen of supplements could be tailored to that child's nutritional needs and symptom profile. In reality, however, most nutritional deficiencies are assumed rather than established by laboratory analysis. Many supplements are marketed in combination formulas that take a "one size fits all" approach.

Some dietary supplements can have interactions with other medications or prior conditions, so it is wise to consult a doctor before undertaking dietary supplementation. If commercial supplements are used, parents are encouraged to introduce one supplement at a time, taking careful notes about behavior. Adhere to recommended doses for consumption, as many supplements are toxic at high doses.[3]

WHAT WILL YOU READ ON THE INTERNET ABOUT DIETARY SUPPLEMENTS AS A TREATMENT FOR ASD?

There are many websites devoted to ASD claiming that dietary supplements are a critical treatment for ASD. Some websites even assert that supplements will completely cure ASD. Many of these websites, however, are affiliated with individuals or companies who sell supplements. Note that the FDA does not allow manufacturers of dietary supplements to make claims that their supplements cure or even treat any disorder or disease, including ASD. At most, manufacturers are permitted to make suggestions that their supplements may improve certain behaviors or conditions. This does not, however, prevent retail sellers of those same supplements from making unsubstantiated claims.

More moderate websites, such as Talk About Curing Autism (TACA: www.tacanow.org), discuss the possibility that supplements can improve the general well-being of a person diagnosed with ASD. Most of the evidence is in the form of testimonials from families of children with ASD who have implemented dietary supplements and have found that certain behaviors, such as speech, eye contact, behavioral compliance and sleeping patterns, have improved for their children.

Information that is available online about individual supplements is frequently contradictory. For example, one website reports that vitamin B6 improves symptoms of ASD without describing how, while another website claims that children should not take vitamin B6 because of the serious health risks associated with it (e.g., neuropathy). Other reports advise that vitamin B6 works only when taken with magnesium.

Many families use dietary supplements in conjunction with each other, as well as in combination with other dietary and behavioral treatments. For example, many people who use supplements to improve behaviors of children with ASD also use a gluten-free/casein-free diet, as well as behavioral therapies such as Applied Behavioral Analysis. As such, it may be impossible to determine which intervention is responsible for improving a particular symptom or behavior.

WHAT DO SCIENTISTS SAY ABOUT DIETARY SUPPLEMENTS?

Of the dozens of available dietary supplements, only a few have been scientifically researched as treatments for ASD. Of the most widely used supplements, melatonin, fatty acids, vitamin C and dimethylglycine (DMG) have been the most studied. When reviewing the evidence in favor of dietary supplements as a treatment for ASD, it is very important to note that these studies show placebo response rates of more than 30 percent! This means that about one-third of families of children with ASD report improvement in a child's behavior even when the child is not taking an actual supplement. Such findings demonstrate that there is a strong power of suggestion and expectation associated with dietary supplements that may overestimate the actual effectiveness of supplements in treating ASD. In a placebo control study, one group of people takes a particular supplement, while another group takes an inactive sugar pill (a placebo). A placebo response rate is a measure of the power of suggestion and expectation. How many of the sugar-pill takers report improvements in symptoms? In studies of nutritional supplements for ASD, about one-third of families whose children are taking sugar pills report noticing positive improvements in function.

In 2009, a researcher conducted a thorough review of previous studies examining supplements for treating ASD.[2] Treatments were "graded" based on the quantity and quality of scientific evidence supporting their effectiveness. Only melatonin received the top grade of A (indicating that there is good scientific evidence for its effectiveness). Several supplements used to treat ASD received nearly failing grades: probiotics and digestive enzymes, TMG (trimethylglycine), DMG, folic acid and vitamin B12.[4, 5, 6, 7, 8, 9] Vitamin B6 plus magnesium and fatty acids received mid-range grades for scientific evidence in spite of the very strong testimonial evidence found on the internet. The supplements with the best scientific evidence for effectiveness in treating the symptoms of ASD are the following:

- **Melatonin** (dose = 1–10 mg/day) has been found to improve sleep patterns and reduce sleep latency in approximately 80 percent of all children with ASD studied. Mild adverse effects have been reported. These include morning drowsiness, pre-bedtime excitement or agitation, increased nighttime waking and increased bedwetting.

- **L-carnitine** (dose = 100 mg/kg/day) has, through controlled studies, been shown to bring about improvements in sleep, energy level and communication skills in children with Rett syndrome. Adverse effects include diarrhea and fishy body odor.

- **BH4** (tetrahydrobiopterin) (dose = 1–3 mg/kg/day) was studied in 14 children with ASD over a 24-week period. Half of the children showed improvements in language and social interaction. In a larger study, half of the 136 individuals with ASD studied reported increases in social interaction, eye contact and vocabulary.

- **Vitamin C** (dose $= 114$ mg/kg/day) resulted in significantly reduced stereotypical behaviors (such as rocking, spinning, pacing, flapping) for 18 children with ASD who participated in a 30-week crossover study. No adverse effects were noted.

While there is some evidence that supplements can help alleviate some of the symptoms typically seen in children with ASD, remember that there are limitations with some of these studies (e.g., not including control groups, not accounting for other therapies or treatments). With a few exceptions, it is difficult to safely and validly say whether most commonly used supplements improve ASD symptoms in children.

WHAT ARE THE COSTS OF DIETARY SUPPLEMENTS?

Generally, bottles of supplements come in monthly rations and costs range widely—from $5 to over $50 per supplement per month. Proponents of supplements support taking supplements indefinitely (i.e., they are not a short-term solution). Specific laboratory testing for nutritional deficiencies is not often covered by insurance. Trial and error approaches to identifying supplements can lead to many unfinished supplies. Medical supervision is wise, because many dietary supplements are toxic in high doses. For example, too much vitamin C can cause gastrointestinal disturbances; too much vitamin D can cause a buildup of calcium resulting in hypercalcemia, while too much iron can be fatal in children.[10] The use of dietary supplements to treat ASD can require a high investment of parental effort. Supplements must be taken on a regular schedule to have an effect (missing doses, or an on again/off again approach are thought to undermine effectiveness). Children are often unable to swallow pills or capsules, and training children with ASD to do so can be especially challenging. The liquid and powdered forms of supplements are usually unpalatable, and need to be hidden in preferred foods and beverages.

DIETARY SUPPLEMENTS

Ages	→	all ages		
Anecdotal parental support	→	not much	mixed	positive
Scientific evidence	→	weak	moderate	strong
Availability	→	limited	moderate	wide
Cost (time and money)	→	minimal	moderate	high

9
GLUTEN-FREE/ CASEIN-FREE DIET

Elisabeth Hollister Sandberg
and Susan E. Michelson

WHAT IS A GLUTEN-FREE/CASEIN-FREE DIET?

A gluten-free/casein-free (GFCF) diet is one in which all gluten and casein are eliminated from the diet. Gluten is a protein that is found in wheat, barley, rye and oats, and any products made from these grains such as food starches, malt, soy sauce, some flavorings and artificial colors. Casein is a protein found in milk. Butter, cheese, yogurt, cream and ice cream all contain casein. Casein is also an ingredient in many processed foods, such as lunchmeats, hot dogs, canned tuna, non-dairy whipped toppings, artificial butter or margarine, and fast foods such as French fries.

HOW DOES A GLUTEN-FREE/CASEIN-FREE DIET SUPPOSEDLY WORK AS A TREATMENT FOR ASD?

The GFCF diet has been used as an intervention for behavioral and mental disorders since the 1960s. There are two different sets of motivations for using a GFCF diet as a treatment for ASD. The first is based on the idea of food sensitivity. Many parents of children with ASD have observed that their children seem to be sensitive to certain foods. These parents often experiment with different diets for their children that involve eliminating particular foods or ingredients. The belief is that when they are relieved of digestive discomfort and pain, children with ASD may become more communicative, may exhibit less disruptive behavior and may sleep better.

The second rationale for using a GFCF diet to treat ASD relates to the Opioid-Excess Theory.[1] It has been proposed that children with ASD may have more difficulty digesting the peptide groups formed by gluten and casein compared to other children. These peptide groups supposedly cross into the bloodstream from the intestines, and then act on the brain the same way that Opioids do. (Opioids include the drugs morphine, heroin and codeine.) So, if children with ASD have undigested peptide groups from gluten and casein, they may impact their brains in a way similar to taking drugs such as heroin, causing them to exhibit behaviors associated with taking those drugs. Opioid-Excess Theory is said to account for symptoms of ASD such as decreased sensitivity to pain (as evidenced by self-injurious behavior) and the need for "sameness" (as evidenced by ritualistic or stereotypic behaviors). Further, some scientists hypothesize that long-term exposure of these peptides in the brain can lead to malformation of brain regions related to social awkwardness and isolation, much in the way that long-term drug abuse can. Theoretically, by removing gluten and casein from the diet, a child will no longer be under the influence of these peptide chains and behaviors associated with opioid use will decrease.

WHAT WILL YOU READ ON THE INTERNET ABOUT A GLUTEN-FREE/CASEIN-FREE DIET AS A TREATMENT FOR ASD?

Because the Opioid-Excess Theory is not widely accepted, there is a great deal of controversy surrounding the use of the GFCF diet to treat ASD, resulting in highly polarized informational websites. As is true with many interventions that require a tremendous amount of commitment from parents, both supporters and detractors vehemently assert their positions. For example, in response to the skepticism of the GFCF diet often voiced by the medical community, the Gluten-free Casein-free website (gfcf.com) boldly states: "Parent surveys done by The Autism Research Institute list the GFCF Diet as one of the most Successful Interventions for the Treatment of Autistic Spectrum Disorders." The website suggests that parents pressure their medical professionals to learn more about the diet and advocate for support in their decision to treat their child with the GFCF diet. A common theme across websites that support the GFCF diet is that it is reasonable to use a treatment that has anecdotal support before it has been identified in the medical literature as an effective treatment. There is a prevailing "you have nothing to lose and everything to gain" sentiment.

There are vast numbers of online "success stories"— testimonials and anecdotal evidence from parents who found GFCF diets to be helpful for their children with ASD. Some parents report that their children display "miraculous" symptom alleviation after a few days on the GFCF diet; for example, their children become happier, can play independently, and have improved eye contact. Some parents report that their nonverbal children started talking after only a few days on the diet.

Digging a little deeper online will reveal more measured websites wherein authors are careful in stating that gluten and casein proteins *might* be responsible for ASD behaviors. Elsewhere, one finds parental reports describing challenges associated with keeping a child on a GFCF diet. Children with ASD are often highly "finicky" eaters. Gluten and casein are common ingredients in most "kid" foods—cereal, crackers, noodles, yogurt and so forth. Eliminating these foods from the finicky eater's diet can be quite difficult—especially if the child is young, or has communication difficulties. Maintaining a GFCF diet "out in the world" adds additional layers of difficulty. Parents typically need to send or bring special foods to school, and options will be highly limited at restaurants and social gatherings. As children get older and consume food outside the watchful gaze of a parent, compliance can be extremely difficult to ensure.

Although a GFCF diet is usually discussed online as a treatment for ASD, gluten-free diets are followed for other conditions such as Celiac disease—resulting in a tremendous amount of online reference material. There are websites that focus on tips and products, those that explain the medical issues, and those that specifically address GFCF diet as an ASD treatment.

Many internet search results lead to websites that sell GFCF products. For example, the GFCF Diet website (www.gfcfdiet.com) provides information on "Getting Started on the Gluten Free/Casein Free Diet," cookbooks, cooking tips and a community bulletin board. It is easy to find lists of foods that do or do not contain gluten or casein. Readers can find websites dedicated to helping to navigate the financial costs of a GFCF diet. For example, Talk About Curing Autism (www.tacanow.org) includes a webpage entitled "GFCFSF Diet on a Budget." Here, authors break down the diet into three approaches delineated by dollar signs: from $$$ = "buy everything premade" down to $ = "cook everything yourself." This website, like many others, also contains links to information about reading ingredient labels, hidden sources of gluten and casein, GFCF shopping lists and companies that carry GFCF products.

WHAT DO SCIENTISTS SAY ABOUT A GLUTEN-FREE/CASEIN-FREE DIET?

In evaluating the GFCF diet as a treatment for ASD, researchers must be careful not to include cases of children with ASD who have medically verified food allergies to wheat and/or dairy. Those conditions are considered to be medical causes for a restricted diet and improvements in health and behavior would be expected on those grounds alone.

Interest in using GFCF diets to treat behavioral and mental disorders began in the mid-1960s when it was noted that the incidence of schizophrenia was low for South Pacific Island societies that had diets low in wheat and dairy. The hypothesis as it pertained to schizophrenia stated that those with the disorder had a genetic defect that prevented them from metabolizing gluten and casein. In 1979, the idea was expanded to include ASD.[2] The logic was based upon animal studies showing that opiate-treated guinea pigs and baby chicks do not fully appreciate pain, do not cry normally, do not cling to parents, do not desire social companionship and show extreme behavioral persistence.

Because of methodological and practical issues, only a small number of studies have scientifically investigated the efficacy of a GFCF diet for ASD. It is very difficult to assess whether a GFCF diet has been effective because of the impact that parental expectations can have on reported outcomes. As hopeful and invested parents very much want the diet to work, they often report improvements in their autistic child's behavior that, when examined objectively, may represent only wishful thinking. A second major problem plaguing the research in this area is one of sample sizes. It is difficult to generalize results when a very small number of participants are used in a study. Scientific conclusions cannot be drawn from the experiences of one or two families. Additionally, the fact that most families of children with ASD are utilizing multiple therapeutic approaches makes it very difficult to assign "credit" for improvements to the diet in particular. Further complicating the ability to draw conclusions is the fact that ASD symptomatology changes as children develop, regardless of intervention.

A good scientific study of the effectiveness of a GFCF diet would ideally compare two groups of equivalent individuals—one group that is on the diet, and one that is not. As we described in more detail in Chapter 2, the gold standard in scientific research is a study in which no one working with the participants knows which of the two groups is which (this takes care of what we call the placebo effect, where parents or researchers see what they expect to see). To date there has been only one such study of the use of the GFCF diet in children with ASD.[3] In 2006, 15 children ages 2–16 years diagnosed with ASD were chosen as study participants. The children consumed only the meals and snacks provided by the researchers for 12 weeks. Half of the children ate a GFCF diet for six weeks, and then a regular diet for six weeks. The other half started with a regular diet for six weeks and then shifted to a GFCF diet. The study was double-blind: neither the investigators nor the parents and children knew which diet they were consuming.

The researchers measured several different outcomes. To test the Opioid-Excess Theory, they measured the urinary peptide excretion levels. Assuming the GFCF was affecting the children as intended, those on the GFCF diet should have had evidence of lower levels of peptide in their urine. No difference was found in these levels when the children were on regular diets versus GFCF diets. Behaviors such as initiation of interaction, responsiveness and intelligible words spoken were also assessed using the Childhood Autism Rating Scale and by research assistants' in-home behavioral observations. These behaviors did not differ depending on the children's diets.[3]

A review of all of the studies of the efficacy of GFCF supports the null conclusions of the study described above. In 2010 a group of researchers reviewed 14 different studies (and then later included a newly published fifteenth study) that had investigated the effectiveness of a GFCF diet for improving ASD behaviors such as communication, stereotypy, play, self-injury and aggression.[4] The size of the groups studied ranged from one to 50, the majority of participants were male (67%) and the range of ages was broad (2–17 years). The length of time the diets were implemented ranged from four days to four years. The average length of diet intervention was ten months. Behavioral outcome data were collected using combinations of questionnaires, direct observation and standardized tests. Some of the studies also measured urinary peptides, enzymes and antibodies. Upon reviewing all of the studies, the researchers concluded that the use of GFCF diets for the treatment of ASD is not supported by scientific evidence. They explain that studies finding positive effects often contain measurement procedures that are greatly influenced by the expectations of participating parents.

There is some evidence that GFCF diets may have potentially harmful consequences. A 2003 study found that children with ASD on a GFCF diet displayed higher deficiencies in certain essential amino acids compared with children with ASD who were not on restricted diets.[5] The researchers concluded that further investigation is essential to determine whether or not restricted diets might place children with ASD at risk for malnutrition that could further impact brain development. A study in 2008 examined bone thickness in 75 young boys with ASD. Boys on casein-free diets showed nearly double the deficiencies in bone thickness than those without restricted diets.[6] These researchers conclude that bone development should be monitored especially closely in boys with ASD who are on restricted diets.

Overall, the scientific data on the utility and effectiveness of the GFCF diet for the treatment of ASD is very weak. The National Autism Center's National Standards Project listed the GFCF diet as an "unestablished treatment" in 2009—meaning there is little to no evidence in support of its effectiveness as a treatment for ASD.[7]

WHAT ARE THE COSTS OF A GLUTEN-FREE/CASEIN-FREE DIET?

There are potentially significant health costs (malnutrition, loss of bone density) associated with the GFCF diet. Parents should implement a GFCF diet under the supervision and regular monitoring of a physician.

The basics of a GFCF diet are meats and produce that tend to be more costly grocery items than grain-based foods. Specially prepared GFCF foods (crackers, cereal) can be quite expensive, often two to three times the cost of a regular product containing gluten or casein. Foods free of both gluten and casein can be difficult to find, though commercial availability of GFCF foods has increased dramatically in recent years. Because it can be difficult to locate GFCF foods in local grocery stores, especially in rural areas, some families rely on mail-order foods. GFCF diet websites suggest investing in "starter manuals" (with a price range of $30–60) and special cookbooks.

There are effort and social costs to GFCF diets as well. Parents should plan for regular consultations with their child's doctors to verify adequate nutrition. Policing the food consumption of one family member, or changing the dietary habits of the entire family, can cause a great deal of strain. Most children strongly resist the dietary changes. The need to scrutinize labels means that grocery shopping and food preparation require additional time. Dining at restaurants or in friends' homes usually means bringing along separate, special food for the child. Birthday parties, school functions and other social activities featuring food present a host of challenges for the child with dietary restrictions.

GLUTEN-FREE/CASEIN-FREE (GFCF) DIET

Ages	→	all ages		
Anecdotal parental support	→	not much	mixed	positive
Scientific evidence	→	weak	moderate	strong
Availability	→	limited	moderate	wide
Cost (time and money)	→	minimal	moderate	high

10

HYPERBARIC OXYGEN THERAPY

Nicholas D. Taylor and
Elisabeth Hollister Sandberg

WHAT IS HYPERBARIC OXYGEN THERAPY?

Hyperbaric Oxygen Therapy (HBOT) refers to the practice of sitting or lying inside a special chamber (usually a horizontally oriented cylinder) while an air mixture is mechanically pumped into it, increasing the atmospheric pressure and oxygen content within the chamber. HBOT is used to treat conditions requiring or benefiting from increased availability of oxygen in bodily tissues such as altitude sickness, carbon monoxide poisoning and wounds from burns. HBOT began to emerge as an increasingly popular treatment for ASD in the early 2000s.

HOW DOES HYPERBARIC OXYGEN THERAPY SUPPOSEDLY WORK AS A TREATMENT FOR ASD?

Hyperbaric Oxygen Therapy is a legitimate medical treatment approved by the FDA for a limited number of conditions.[1] Patients are placed in a strong, steel chamber that allows the atmospheric pressure around them to be increased while exposing them to pure or elevated levels of oxygen. The increased oxygen and pressure dramatically increases oxygen transport by blood plasma during treatment. For decompression sickness (divers experience this if they ascend to the surface of the water too quickly), HBOT is used to "recompress" and restore blood oxygen levels. For some other conditions, such as burns and skin grafts, HBOT is useful because it can increase the oxygen available to damaged body tissues not receiving adequate blood flow, delaying tissue death.[2]

Advocates of HBOT as a treatment for ASD assert that individuals with ASD may benefit from HBOT for three reasons. First, proponents note that research studies have shown that some individuals with ASD have reduced blood flow to certain areas of the brain (such as the thalamus, the temporal lobes, the amygdala and others). Reduced blood flow to these areas is said to result in impairments in emotional expression, desire for sameness, repetitive behaviors and decreased IQ.[3] Second, research is often cited indicating that children with ASD have increased neural inflammation and gastrointestinal inflammation (swelling). Inflamed tissues can cause pain and interfere with the proper function of those body parts. Third, advocates state that ASD is characterized by increased oxidative stress—an imbalance between the production and use of chemically reactive molecules containing oxygen; this imbalance can lead to cell damage. HBOT is offered as an intervention that may help individuals with ASD by increasing blood flow to the brain, decreasing neural and gastric inflammation, and reducing oxidative stress that could be damaging brain tissue. Additionally, some proponents have suggested that HBOT may also mobilize stem cells that could work to repair damaged areas of the brain, restoring functioning and improving ASD symptoms.[4]

WHAT WILL YOU READ ON THE INTERNET ABOUT HYPERBARIC OXYGEN THERAPY AS A TREATMENT FOR ASD?

Hyperbaric Oxygen Therapy has become increasingly prominent within the popular literature on ASD treatment. An internet search about the intervention reveals a large number of news articles, blog posts, descriptions and videos offering information and commentary. These sources range from sensational news reports to highly detailed commentaries on the treatment's validity by knowledgeable medical doctors. Given the controversial nature of using HBOT to treat ASD, consumers looking for information will encounter a combination of adamant supporters and strong critics. Overall, parents and consumers interested in HBOT for ASD will find an overwhelming amount of information about the treatment online. The sources vary dramatically in their emphasis, quality and conclusions, with some individuals proclaiming it a cure, and others concluding that it is an unlikely, or at least a purely speculative treatment. Many of the influential ASD organizations providing information about treatments mention HBOT as a possible therapy. For instance, the Association for Science in Autism Treatment provides a very brief descriptive summary of the research and states, "there have been no studies with strong experimental designs" on HBOT for ASD. They recommend that professionals present the treatment as untested.[5] Other organizations don't even mention the treatment, such as the Autism Speaks website (www.autismspeaks.org). Still others provide a large of amount of information supportive of the treatment. In general, organizations and ASD news websites that emphasize evidence and science-based interventions treat HBOT with skepticism. The popular Left-Brain Right-Brain blog would be an example. Organizations and websites that emphasize alternative medical treatments, such as Natural News and the Autism Research Institute, have been advocates of the treatment. The Autism Research Institute's website (www.autism.com) prominently features HBOT at the top of a list of "noteworthy treatments that help some autistic children." In summary, depending on where you look, writers provide very different accounts of the effectiveness of HBOT as an ASD treatment.

Coverage in the news media also varies in perspective. Some writers focus on the potential of HBOT and will cover the story of a child currently undergoing the treatment. These articles quote the treatment provider describing how HBOT works, and also interview the child's parents about the impact that treatment has had on the child. These sources tend to emphasize the possibility of therapeutic benefit, provide anecdotal accounts of improvement from practitioners and parents, and occasionally mention that it is a controversial treatment. Readers may also encounter news sources that emphasize new research or the scientific basis of the treatment. These articles may cover technical aspects of the research associated with HBOT for ASD, such as whether the research is of good quality. These sources tend to be more critical of HBOT for ASD than local or national news stories that focus on practitioners and individual stories. Similar articles that delve even deeper into the science behind HBOT can provide interested consumers with extremely detailed accounts and explanation of the research underlying HBOT's popularization and controversy.

Many websites have been created by individual practitioners and clinics who profit by offering HBOT services for ASD. One Defeat Autism Now practitioner maintains a website largely focused on HBOT.[6] On his website, he offers information about how HBOT works, conditions it may treat, and an online shop where you can order your own hyperbaric chamber at significant expense. He offers claims about his ability to treat ASD as well as parents' testimonials reporting remarkable symptom reversals in treated children.

WHAT DO SCIENTISTS SAY ABOUT HYPERBARIC OXYGEN THERAPY?

The use of HBOT as a treatment for ASD is based on the beliefs that neuro-inflammation, intestinal inflammation, oxidative stress and poor blood flow in the brain are probable causes of ASD symptoms, and that HBOT can alleviate these problems. While there is indeed scientific evidence of reduced or abnormal blood flow in some areas of some ASD children's brains, researchers are unsure about how to interpret such findings. The neuro-inflammation evidence comes from a research team at Johns Hopkins University. Because these researchers felt their work was being repeatedly misused to justify a variety of treatments (such as HBOT), they have produced some FAQs regarding their work on neuro-inflammation among individuals with ASD.[7] They note that the neural inflammatory responses may be a system of protection and repair for the brain, not a problem requiring intervention. Additionally, they note that ASD is "highly variable in the way it presents...it is possible that our sample of cases does not represent the entire autistic spectrum."

In 2006 a collection of case reports was published that described the effects of HBOT for six children with ASD. Across these individualized cases, promising results emerged.[8] In 2007 the same researchers studied 18 children and adolescents with ASD using a more rigorous comparison group design.[9] Children were assigned to one of two treatment groups that differed in the amount of pressure and oxygen to which they were exposed over 40 treatment sessions. One group received pressure and oxygen levels of HBOT, the other group received pressure and oxygen that were only slightly higher than regular "room air." The researchers compared the two groups on a variety of relevant measures including biological indicators of oxidative stress and behavioral measures such as motivation, speech and cognitive awareness. Treatment results were mixed. Biological indicators of oxidative stress were not meaningfully different for either group. Parents of children in the HBOT group, however, reported perceiving improvements in the areas of motivation, speech and cognitive awareness.[9] Unfortunately, it is impossible to rule out other potential explanations for the results. Parents were not blind to the group to which their children were assigned. In other words, they knew whether or not their child was receiving HBOT. Because all measures of symptoms were based on parent reports, rather than independent, objective testing, the potential for parental expectations to color perceptions of effectiveness was high.

Another study published by this research team in 2009 was the first "double-blind, placebo controlled study" of HBOT for ASD and is widely cited as evidence in support of using HBOT to treat ASD.[10] Researchers studied 62 children with ASD ranging in age from two to seven years. Children were randomly assigned to one of two groups: one received increased pressure and increased oxygen (the HBOT group), the other received only slightly increased pressure (the control group). The children in the HBOT group showed improvements in ASD symptoms such as receptive language, social interaction and eye contact. Problematically, other researchers have been unable to replicate the results from this study, and some have argued that the method of data analysis was flawed.

Other studies have failed to confirm previous positive findings about the effectiveness of HBOT as an ASD treatment. In 2010 a study was conducted comparing HBOT to a placebo for 34 children with ASD ages 2–14.[11] This study found no difference between the HBOT and placebo groups for either observational measures of behavioral symptoms or any of several standardized tests of functioning. A 2011 study used a multiple baseline design to study the effects of HBOT on the ASD symptoms of 16 children.[12] In this type of design, repeated measurements of behavior are made for each individual child, thereby allowing the researchers to examine individual changes in behavior corresponding with the treatment sessions. Trends in behavior are then compared across the times when the child is receiving each treatment (or, as in this study, over the time when the child was receiving "official" HBOT compared to when the child was receiving a mild oxygen and pressure treatment). The researchers found no consistent effect of HBOT on a wide array of behaviors related to social functioning, verbal skills and problematic behaviors.

In sum, a series of initial studies suggested potentially promising results, but more recent work has not confirmed those findings. Taken as a whole, the scientific research does not currently suggest that HBOT is effective for alleviating ASD symptoms.

WHAT ARE THE COSTS OF HYPERBARIC OXYGEN THERAPY?

HBOT intervention protocols for ASD involve 40 or more one-hour sessions at typical cost of $100 per session. Use of HBOT to treat ASD is not covered by insurance. Some consumers of HBOT opt to rent or purchase their own soft-shell chambers. The price for a portable chamber ranges from

$6000 to $16,000 and a physician's prescription is required. HBOT is generally considered to be a safe procedure, but there is a small risk of serious health consequences such as organ damage or seizures. All medical equipment utilizing oxygen presents a serious fire hazard. Medical facilities are built according to codes and governed by strict regulations to ensure the safe operation of such equipment. Fire hazard should be a factor of strong concern for anyone using HBOT outside of an official medical facility.

HYPERBARIC OXYGEN THERAPY (HBOT)

Ages	→	all ages		
Anecdotal parental support	→	not much	mixed	positive
Scientific evidence	→	weak	moderate	strong
Availability	→	limited	moderate	wide
Cost (time and money)	→	minimal	moderate	high

11

THE MILLER METHOD

Mary Beth McCullough and
Elisabeth Hollister Sandberg

WHAT IS THE MILLER METHOD?

The Miller Method is a cognitive-developmental approach to treatment that focuses on four main issues often seen in children with ASD: problems with body coordination, social interactions, communication skills and symbolic reasoning. The Miller Method emphasizes an integrated approach to treatment, wherein children are guided through exercises targeting several areas of functioning to transform children's disruptive behaviors into functional ones. It is an action-oriented therapy, encouraging children to move their entire bodies and to make direct, physical contact with objects and people while engaging in activities. This intervention is taught by certified Miller Method professionals, and can be applied in numerous settings (home, school or clinic).

HOW DOES THE MILLER METHOD SUPPOSEDLY WORK AS A TREATMENT FOR ASD?

Founded in 1965 by Dr. Arnold Miller and his wife Eileen Eller-Miller, the Miller Method is guided by a cognitive-developmental systems approach, a theory based on the

Millers' clinical experience as well as research from historical influential developmental theorists such as Piaget. The main premise is that children develop important skills and abilities through their continuous and active involvement with the environment. Children learn "systems," or organized chunks of behaviors, that become more complex and controlled as they develop. For example, when children are first introduced to an object such as a wagon, they might push and pull the wagon repetitively without fully understanding what they are doing. However, as their system for pushing and pulling develops, they begin to understand what the words "push" and "pull" mean, and they can control their movement of the wagon accordingly.

As a treatment for ASD, the Miller Method assumes that children with ASD are "stuck" in earlier stages of cognitive development, and thus have impaired functioning.[1] The Miller Method maintains that children with ASD have not fully developed systems, and therefore, they may engage in repetitive behaviors because they are not fully connecting their actions with the world around them (i.e., not connecting the words "push" and "pull" with their movement of the wagon). Importantly, this theory asserts that children with ASD have the capacity to relate to the world around them; they just have not developed the systems to do so yet. Miller Method therapists seek to determine the purpose behind disordered behavior and then attempt to transform that disordered behavior into functional behavior. Efforts focus on finding ways to encourage social and communicative skills that replace the "closed ways of being" that are characteristic of children with ASD.

The main goal of the Miller Method is to guide the child through the development of four main systems of behavior:

- **Body coordination:** integrating sensory and motor capacities to reach a certain goal.

- **Social interactions:** improving social behaviors such as turn-taking, competing or bonding.

- **Communication skills:** integrating words, actions and objects in relationships to another person.

- **Symbolic reasoning:** organizing the relation between symbols and what they represent.

Recommended treatment begins with an in-depth assessment to determine the level of the child's existing systems. Miller Method therapists subsequently introduce activities targeting the child's developmental level to fill gaps in their systems.

A key tool used in the Miller Method treatment is a piece of equipment called the "elevated square." The elevated square is a wooden platform that is raised 2.5 feet (76 cm) off the ground, with steps on both sides of the platform for the child to climb up and down. While on the elevated square, children are encouraged to complete activities focused on improving social interaction, communication and symbolic reasoning skills. The Millers started using elevation when they observed that children became more aware of their bodies, produced better eye contact, and were more focused and better able to learn while on elevated structures.[2]

Narration and sign language are other key techniques used in the Miller Method. The therapist narrates and signs what the child is doing while he or she is doing it to facilitate the child's awareness of the connection between words, actions and the world around him or her. Another Miller Method strategy introduces children to disorganization and disruption to help them learn how to manage transitions and become more flexible. Therapists may engage in behaviors such as interrupting children in the middle of an activity, or placing obstacles along their path on the elevated square, to guide them through managing change and disorder flexibly and effectively. For children without ASD, challenges to their systems cause children to spontaneously adjust and adapt their systems. Children with ASD, however, need a lot of help making changes to their systems.

WHAT WILL YOU READ ON THE INTERNET ABOUT THE MILLER METHOD AS A TREATMENT FOR ASD?

Even though it was developed in the 1960s, the Miller Method is not a particularly high profile therapeutic intervention for ASD. Finding independent basic descriptions of the treatment is difficult. Few nutshell descriptions or evaluations are available. Most websites, books and articles contain complex language about the treatment and can be difficult for the average reader to navigate and understand. The few websites that do provide basic information often do not explain the reasons behind the defining features of the Miller Method (in particular the elevated square). It is worth noting that although the Miller Method does not have a heavy online "buzz," there is also no significant online opposition.

One source that does provide a thorough and descriptive explanation of this treatment is the official Miller Method website.[3] This website details the treatment's goals, explains the cognitive-developmental systems approach and provides specific information about pricing and treatment options. Pictures of the elevated square and other techniques used in this treatment are also available on the website. This website contains glowing parental testimonials ("There is not enough I can say about these wonderful people [the Miller Method therapists] that have virtually saved my son from a life of mere existence to one of meaning and purpose") to broad claims about this treatment's effectiveness which may not be supported by research (see below).

WHAT DO SCIENTISTS SAY ABOUT
THE MILLER METHOD?

Thus far, only two published studies have examined the effectiveness of the Miller Method.[2, 4] The authors of both studies concluded that the Miller Method improves children's language comprehension and expression, communication skills and pragmatic competence (the ability to understand another speaker's meaning). A closer look at both studies, though, shows that children's gains may be influenced by factors other than the treatment.

In the mid-1970s the Millers themselves conducted the first study examining the effectiveness of the Miller Method, with 19 nonverbal individuals ranging in age from six to 20 years who were diagnosed with moderate to severe ASD.[2] Each individual received treatment for one hour a day, five days a week, for approximately 13 months. Before treatment, none of the young people in the study were able to use words or sign language to express themselves; however, after treatment, all 19 individuals could respond to signs paired with spoken words, and also to spoken words without signs. Expressive language was more difficult for the young people to acquire, with only 36 percent of the sample able to use spoken words following treatment.

Similar results were found in a case study that followed one 33-month-old "severely autistic" boy while he received the Miller Method.[4] The treatment was delivered for two and a half hours a day, four days a week, for five months. After five months of intervention, the child showed small gains in language expression and comprehension, social interaction and play, dressing, feeding and pragmatic competence.

Thus, it might appear that the Miller Method does benefit children with severe forms of ASD, particularly in the areas of language comprehension and expression. However, the studies have limitations to consider when evaluating the results. Neither study measured the other important "systems" of functioning that the Millers believe are essential (e.g., body coordination, social interaction) before and after treatment to see if there were any changes. The first study used a small sample of children with severe ASD and the second study followed the progress of a single child so the results may not apply to the wider ASD population. Neither study compared the Miller Method treatment to a comparison treatment or control group (a group of children who did not receive the Miller Method treatment). Therefore, we do not know if other factors such as increased attention from adults or basic development over time might explain the findings. The researchers were involved in the center that promotes and sells the Miller Method services. In science this is called a "conflict of interest" (see Chapter 2). Independent investigation is essential to truly establish the validity of the results.

Thus far, the positive findings provide a base from which future research should build, but we cannot confidently state that the Miller Method is an effective method for improving functioning in children with ASD.

WHAT ARE THE COSTS OF THE MILLER METHOD?

There are several different components to the Miller Method, each carrying a different cost. The Miller Method Diagnostic Survey is an assessment that the parent or caregiver completes online about the child's behavior in relation to body organization, social contact, communication and symbolic reasoning skills. The answers are sent to an examiner in the Miller Method Language and Development Center (LCDC), after which a report with recommendations is sent to the parent or caregiver. The fee for this survey is $100, with additional costs accrued if the parent purchases the Miller Method equipment recommended by the examiner.

The Miller Umwelt Assessment is a more in-depth assessment that is conducted only at the LCDC in Massachusetts. It is a two-hour assessment during which an examiner assesses the level of the child's systems. After the assessment, parents receive a videotaped copy of the assessment, as well as a detailed written report with recommendations. The fee for the Miller Umwelt Assessment is $1000, plus any expenses associated with traveling to the center.

The Parent-Child Training program takes place at the LCDC in Massachusetts for approximately 12 hours over the course of three days. It begins with a Miller Umwelt Assessment, and the recommendations from this assessment are tested during the second and third day. The examiners help to develop a home or school-based program for the child at the conclusion of training. The fee for this package is $3750, plus the costs associated with traveling to the center.

For those who cannot travel to the center, distance consultation is offered via video, phone or internet conferencing. A typical videoconferencing contract costs $2000 for two one-hour sessions per week over the course of a month.

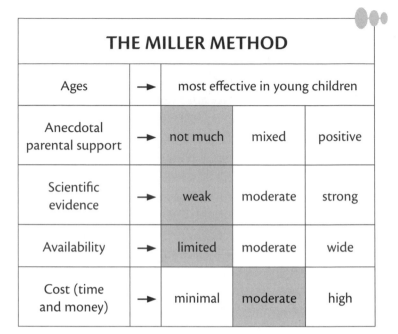

THE MILLER METHOD			
Ages →	most effective in young children		
Anecdotal parental support →	not much	mixed	positive
Scientific evidence →	weak	moderate	strong
Availability →	limited	moderate	wide
Cost (time and money) →	minimal	moderate	high

12

MUSIC THERAPY

Elisabeth Hollister Sandberg
and Katherine K. Bedard

WHAT IS MUSIC THERAPY?

Music Therapy is the use of music within a therapeutic relationship to bring about positive social, emotional, cognitive or physical change in an individual. Unlike musical instruction, the purpose of which is to train musical abilities, Music Therapy does not require musical talent, nor is mastery of musical skill a goal. Music therapists are generally credentialed professionals who have completed approved training programs. Music Therapy as a profession in the United States dates back to the early twentieth century, with the National Association for Music Therapy being created in 1950 as a collaborative organization of professionals who used Music Therapy to treat a variety of individuals, including those with intellectual and psychiatric disabilities.

HOW DOES MUSIC THERAPY SUPPOSEDLY WORK AS A TREATMENT FOR ASD?

Music Therapy is based on the belief that every individual, regardless of a physical, cognitive or emotional disability, has an innate responsiveness to music that can be utilized to enhance well-being. For children with ASD, Music Therapy targets social and communicative deficits associated with the disorder. Collaborating with a trained music "partner"— taking turns and sharing—encourages socialization and communication with requiring verbal language. Many children with ASD show a particular interest in music, making it easy to include Music Therapy as a part of a system of interventions.[1]

Music therapists will use instruments and voices to engage children with ASD in singing and movement activities that are structured to promote skills such as rhythm, listening, turn-taking, matching and sharing. Music therapists work to create a pleasurable, familiar, musical environment that provides positive support for exploration and expression. Music Therapy is considered to be a "creative therapy," and so there are no specified general "lesson plans." One of the hallmarks of Music Therapy is that it is customized for each individual's linguistic, intellectual, social, emotional and musical abilities.

The most widely used form of Music Therapy, Improvisational Music Therapy, relies on spontaneous musical production. Therapists use instruments and their own voices to respond creatively to the sounds produced in the moment by the child, and encourage the child to reciprocate with sounds in his or her own musical "language." In this way, the therapeutic pair develops its own creative language involving music. Through these techniques, the child may gain greater comfort and confidence with different forms of expression, broaden the range of his or her emotional experiences, and gain practice with reciprocal communication. For individuals with ASD, Improvisational Music Therapy may therefore provide a unique opportunity to engage in a two-way, communicative relationship.[1]

Another form of Music Therapy, Musical Interaction Therapy, utilizes interactive play rather than musical improvisation.[2] For children with ASD who are not particularly verbal, Musical Interaction Therapy is used to support preverbal play patterns. Assuming that natural engagement impulses are diminished or absent in children with ASD, Musical Interaction Therapy attempts to elicit sociability through musical play and then develop it into a more sophisticated form of interaction. Live music is synchronized to the adult-child interactions to facilitate communication. Over time, children learn how to anticipate their play partner's actions based upon the synchronicity of the music. Because the music reflects the mood, timing and meaning of the interactive play, children build skills in reciprocal communication and joint attention.

Music Therapy is believed to have particular benefits for people with ASD because essentially no verbal communication is necessary. In addition to improving shared communication skills such as imitation, joint attention and turn-taking, Music Therapy is also believed to increase self-awareness by helping the individual distinguish between self and other. This self-other distinction fosters communication by underscoring the need for social interaction. The playful aspect of Music Therapy may increase a child's sociability by providing the child with positive, reinforcing social interactions. Finally, Music Therapy may also increase an individual's tolerance for sound or noise—hypersensitivity is sometimes found in individuals with ASD.

WHAT WILL YOU READ ON THE INTERNET ABOUT MUSIC THERAPY AS A TREATMENT FOR ASD?

Much of what turns up in an internet search for Music Therapy and ASD are basic informational websites established by Music Therapy associations and programs that explain the qualifications of credentialed music therapists, the theories behind the approach, and examples of what happens during Music Therapy sessions.

An improvisational music therapist is generally expected to have training in both music and the mental health fields. A typical curriculum involves courses in music, psychology, special education and anatomy, with additional coursework and field experiences specific to Music Therapy. Following completion of their coursework, students are required to complete a six-month full-time clinical internship and a written board certification exam. Registered, board certified Music Therapy professionals must maintain continuing education credits or retake the exam to remain up-to-date in the field. Unlike Improvisational Music Therapy, Music Interaction Therapy is less formally regulated as a treatment strategy. Because Music Interaction Therapy utilizes music as a therapeutic "tool" rather than a set of specific therapeutic techniques, formal Music Therapy training is not required.

Music therapists are employed in many different settings including hospitals, mental health agencies, physical rehabilitation centers, nursing homes, public and private schools, substance abuse programs, forensic facilities, hospice programs and day care facilities. In addition, many music therapists are starting private practices in Music Therapy. Parents can contact the Association of Professional Music Therapists (APMT) for help in finding a music therapist working in their area. Many schools offer Music Therapy for children with ASD as part of their everyday curriculum.

There is very little controversy surrounding Music Therapy as a treatment for ASD. Music Therapy is enjoyable, not time consuming, relatively inexpensive and has no known negative side effects. One of the most widely cited advantages of Music Therapy is that it can be used with preverbal or nonverbal individuals. As such, Music Therapy is very positively endorsed by parents and professionals. A study completed in 1992 in Germany found that 56 percent of child psychiatrists recommended Music Therapy for the treatment of ASD, and 25.1 percent of pediatricians considered Music Therapy useful for individuals with ASD.[3] The claims made about positive impact on ASD symptoms are generally modest—you will not find testimonial evidence of "cures" or "transformations." Music Therapy is generally accepted as a useful part of a broader ASD intervention program.

WHAT DO SCIENTISTS SAY ABOUT MUSIC THERAPY?

Historically, research on Music Therapy was based on case studies (see Chapter 2 for a discussion of the limitations of this approach). Since 1990, there have been only twenty published studies that have used controlled designs to assess the effects of Music Therapy on the behaviors of children with ASD. These twenty studies all used very small groups of children—ten or fewer. Although it is impossible to generalize results obtained from one small group, across many small group studies one can see a pattern of evidence in support of the effectiveness of Music Therapy as a useful ASD intervention.

In 2004, one researcher conducted a meta-analysis of nine studies dating back to the mid-1970s.[4] In a meta-analysis, data from many studies are compiled and examined and "big picture" results are extracted. The studies all involved children or adolescents with ASD, and compared music therapy to non-music conditions. Across the nine studies, Music Therapy had a relatively high positive effect regardless of the age of the individuals or the type of music used.

A more recent study in 2007 assessed whether a Music Therapy program would enhance the behavioral profiles of young adults severely affected by ASD.[5] Eight young adults took part in a total of 52 weekly group Music Therapy sessions lasting 60 minutes each. Each session consisted of singing, piano playing and drumming performed by two music therapists who actively engaged the participants in their musical performances. An external therapist who was not involved in the treatment rated each person's overall psychiatric symptoms (irritability, social engagement, adjustment) before treatment began, midway through the treatment and upon completion. Results showed significant improvements in behaviors over the first six months of the program, but no substantial behavioral change in the second six months of the study.

In a 2008 study, researchers compared the joint attention and social communication of ten young children (ages three to five) during Music Therapy sessions and play sessions with toys.[6] Children participated in 12 weekly 30-minute Improvisational Music Therapy sessions and 12 weekly 30-minute play therapy sessions. Analysis of the videotaped sessions showed more eye contact and turn-taking during the Music Therapy sessions than during the play sessions. In a separate study, these researchers demonstrated that children displayed more joy, emotional synchronicity (matching), engagement and compliant responses during Music Therapy sessions than during play sessions. Taken together, these studies indicate the positive effects of Music Therapy during the treatment process.

In 2009 the National Autism Center's National Standards Project rated Music Therapy as an "emerging treatment" for ASD.[7] According to the report, "Emerging Treatments are those for which one or more studies suggest the intervention may produce favorable outcomes." While this is promising, they state that additional high quality studies involving rigorous methodologies (consistent treatment protocols, objective measures of behavior, assessment of long-term outcomes) must be conducted in order to be confident that Music Therapy is a truly effective treatment for ASD.

In sum, there is no evidence that Music Therapy is harmful or produces any negative effects. Most research shows that children with ASD benefit from Music Therapy interventions and show increases in desirable social and communicative behaviors during the intervention sessions. Whether these increases in desirable behaviors persist outside of the Music Therapy session is unknown.

WHAT ARE THE COSTS OF MUSIC THERAPY?

Some schools and social service organizations may provide Music Therapy without fee as a part of a child's educational plan or through community activities. In private settings, the cost of receiving Music Therapy depends on whether the therapy is taking place within a group or an individual setting, as well as the music therapist's level of education and training. Music Therapy sessions are typically held for 30–60 minutes per week for a period of months to years. Most families pay out-of-pocket for private Music Therapy services; insurance plans rarely provide reimbursement for services. Group sessions average around $55 an hour with the costs split between the participants and individual sessions around $60 an hour. Rates are likely to be higher (closer to $90–100 per hour) for therapists with advanced academic degrees.

MUSIC THERAPY

Ages	→	all ages		
Anecdotal parental support	→	not much	mixed	positive
Scientific evidence	→	weak	moderate	strong
Availability	→	limited	moderate	wide
Cost (time and money)	→	minimal	moderate	high

13

P.L.A.Y. PROJECT HOME CONSULTATION PROGRAM

Kirstin Brown Birtwell
and Becky L. Spritz

WHAT IS THE P.L.A.Y. PROJECT HOME CONSULTATION PROGRAM?

The P.L.A.Y. Project Home Consultation (PPHC) program was developed in 2001 by Dr. Richard Solomon as a community-based, parent-delivered, efficient and cost-effective early intervention program for children with ASD. P.L.A.Y.—Play and Language for Autistic Youngsters— refers to the intervention's focus on building relationships through interactions. PPHC uses Dr. Stanley Greenspan's developmental, individualized and relationship-based DIR/ Floortime (see Chapter 7) theory to inform its play-based intervention approach.[1] PPHC is intended for families with children under six years of age with ASD. The program is consistent with the National Research Council recommendations for intensive early intervention (25 hours per week of one-on-one therapy), but provides it at a lower cost than either Floortime or other behavioral programs, such as Applied Behavioral Analysis.

HOW DOES THE P.L.A.Y. PROJECT HOME CONSULTATION PROGRAM SUPPOSEDLY WORK AS A TREATMENT FOR ASD?

Professionals and researchers agree that children with ASD significantly benefit from intensive, comprehensive intervention approaches in which therapists engage with only one or two children, 25 or more hours per week, for two to four years between the ages of 18 months and six years. Because the cost of intensive early interventions can be remarkably high, ranging from $25,000 to $60,000 per year, PPHC was designed to provide a cost-effective way of delivering an intensive structured intervention program that addresses the language, social and behavioral deficits of children with ASD.[2]

PPHC is a comprehensive, intensive and multidisciplinary approach to treating ASD. Using the theoretical framework of DIR/Flootime (see Chapter 7), PPHC is a "train the trainer" program that teaches parents to independently implement techniques for improving the social reciprocity and functional pragmatic communication of their children with ASD. Home-based consultants teach parents ways to interact with their child in ways that promote the child's social functioning and language, while simultaneously building a stronger parent-child bond.

PPHC targets children's challenges with social pragmatics—the subtle skills required to effectively communicate in a variety of situations and with a variety of individuals. Social pragmatics require a child to be able to monitor and modify his or her communications and interactions with others and involves skills such as joint attention and perspective taking—areas of deficit for children with ASD. The important difference between PPHC and Floortime, however, is that PPHC designates the parent as the primary administrator of the therapeutic intervention. Teaching parents the necessary skills to foster children's development provides more opportunities for building positive relationships and is also more cost-effective than having outside therapists working 25 or more hours per week.

PPHC begins with a one-day training workshop for parents to teach them the play-based techniques and strategies that facilitate the development of social pragmatics. The goal is for parents to be able to independently and effectively implement these techniques with their children. Parents learn to provide Floortime sessions (e.g., play periods of 20–30 minutes) and to integrate activities and strategies into naturally occurring daily routines (e.g., mealtime or bedtime). After the initial parent-training workshop, the program also includes monthly home visits that serve as follow-up workshop sessions. These workshops provide individualized continuing education for parents in their roles as primary therapists. During these workshops, consultants review videotapes of recorded sessions with parents. Parents also receive a training manual for future, ongoing reference.

WHAT WILL YOU READ ON THE INTERNET ABOUT THE P.L.A.Y. PROJECT HOME CONSULTATION PROGRAM AS A TREATMENT FOR ASD?

A general internet search for "P.L.A.Y. Project Home Consultation program" yields hundreds of results, comprised of various pages from PPHC's official website, media blurbs and several research databases that contain PPHC's first and only published study, described in greater detail below. These resources often discuss the "cost-effective" aspect of this program, which has made it appealing for professionals and families alike.

The official website for the PPHC program (www. playproject.org) provides detailed information about the theory behind the program, what the program entails, home consulting and training resources, workshop and conference dates, contact information, media segments and articles and parental testimonials. The website presents a persuasive argument for the approach, including claims that, "by doing what your child loves, your child will love being with you." Parents' testimonials on this website generally highlight advancements in children's communication skills and social connections and communication. Parents also report improved sense of agency—feeling as though they are more personally involved in and responsible for fostering their children's development.

Since the early 2000s, PPHC has been used in southeast Michigan, where it originated at the Ann Arbor Center for Developmental and Behavioral Pediatrics clinic. However, PPHC has more recently been introduced to a larger audience and currently serves part of the United States, as well as Canada, England, Ireland, Australia and Switzerland. The Michigan-based PPHC group holds ongoing conferences and agency workshops (see www.playproject. org/homeconsulting_inyourarea.php).

WHAT DO SCIENTISTS SAY ABOUT THE P.L.A.Y. PROJECT HOME CONSULTATION PROGRAM?

Although PPHC is currently taught, disseminated and implemented around the world, the supporting research is surprisingly lacking. Only one clinical trial has been completed to date and it was published by Dr. Solomon who, as creator of the program, can be said to have what scientists call a conflict of interest (see Chapter 2).[2] This study followed 68 children with ASD aged of two to six years and their parents. The children in the sample varied considerably in terms of ASD severity. Families were assessed before and after completing an 8–12 month PPHC program using the Functional Emotional Assessment Scale, a measure containing six subtests directly related to Stanley Greenspan's theory of development (see Chapter 7 on DIR/Floortime). About half of the children made "good" or "very good" functional developmental progress over the study period. Parents reported being very satisfied and stayed engaged in the program, despite its time demands of at least 15 hours per week (25 or more hours per week are recommended).

While the results of this study are promising, this was designated as a "pilot" study—a study that provides preliminary evidence, but which requires further replication, expansion and refinement before making generalized claims about the findings. Of particular note, the pilot study did not include a comparison group of children with ASD who were not participating in the PPHC program, making it impossible to definitively attribute improvements to PPHC rather than to experience with school interventions, simple developmental maturation or a placebo effect. A close examination of the sample reveals that participating families had many other resources; they were generally married, had stable residences and occupations, etc. Because PPHC is, by its very nature, a time-intensive responsibility for parents, its effectiveness might be in part determined by the family's resources. This is an empirical question that requires further investigation, but is a realistic consideration for families contemplating PPHC.

The National Autism Center's National Standards Project rated developmental relationship-based treatments (of which

DIR/Floortime is one) as an "emerging treatment" for ASD in 2009.[3] PPHC, as a Floortime training program, was likewise included in this category. The report cites promising data for these treatments but not enough convincing evidence at the present time to deem the treatments "effective" for children with ASD. In addition to needing more evidence of the effectiveness of Floortime, it has yet to be demonstrated that a supervised "do-it-yourself" Floortime program such PPHC can be equally effective.

The PPHC program received a large grant in 2010 from the National Institute of Mental Health to complete a controlled clinical study of PPHC. The study will compare 60 children with ASD who participate in PPHC with 60 children with ASD who receive standard community interventions. The developmental level, language skills, social skills and sensory-motor profiles of each child will be measured before and after a 12-month intervention period. To administer the study, researchers from the P.L.A.Y. project are partnering with Easter Seals, one of the leading community service providers for individuals with autism. The findings from this study should provide much-needed answers to questions regarding the scientific validity of this intervention for young children with ASD.

WHAT ARE THE COSTS OF THE P.L.A.Y. PROJECT HOME CONSULTATION PROGRAM?

Compared to other treatments that follow the National Research Council recommendations for intensive early intervention, PPHC is a cost-effective treatment package that may be appropriate for a wide range of families. PPHC costs $2500–3000 per year, depending on the number of annual home visits that the family requests. This cost includes the full-day parent workshop, training manual and three- to four-hour monthly home visits or consultation sessions. While the P.L.A.Y. program is designed to be a financially cost-effective treatment program, the time costs may make the treatment less accessible to some families. Parents are required to attend the full-day workshop, coordinate the monthly home visits and also spend a minimum of 15 hours per week (ideally 25 or more hours per week) implementing the program with their child at home.

P.L.A.Y. PROJECT HOME CONSULTATION (PPHC) PROGRAM

Ages	→	most effective in young children		
Anecdotal parental support	→	not much	mixed	positive
Scientific evidence	→	weak	moderate	strong
Availability	→	limited	moderate	wide
Cost (time and money)	→	minimal	moderate	high

14

RELATIONSHIP DEVELOPMENT INTERVENTION

Mary Beth McCullough and
Elisabeth Hollister Sandberg

WHAT IS RELATIONSHIP DEVELOPMENT INTERVENTION?

The Relationship Development Intervention (RDI) was developed by Dr. Steven Gutstein in the 1980s as a parent-based treatment for children and adolescents with ASD. It is considered a cognitive-developmental approach because it addresses some of the core developmental impairments seen in individuals with ASD: impairments in social relationships, emotional functioning, communication, emotional memory, flexible thinking and the simultaneous processing of visual and auditory information. The program focuses on teaching individuals with ASD to evaluate and adapt their behaviors to others in an interactive manner instead of teaching them separate, isolated skills. Parents or caregivers are trained to act as "guides" for the "apprentice" child. The goal is for the apprentice child to eventually learn to share an emotional connection with the parent guide. Developing a shared emotional connection is believed to lead to increased self-awareness, social skills and adaptability necessary to interact with others.

HOW DOES RELATIONSHIP DEVELOPMENT INTERVENTION SUPPOSEDLY WORK AS A TREATMENT FOR ASD?

According to Dr. Gutstein, the core impairments seen in ASD may be the result of impairments in neurological functioning that interfere with the Guided Participation Relationship (GPR) in infancy. GPR refers to a collaborative parent-infant relationship that leads to the infant's development of dynamic intelligence. Dynamic intelligence—the ability to think flexibly, adapt to new situations and take different perspectives—develops in typical children through a cyclical process of parents gradually modifying challenges based on the child's behavior, and the child safely exploring new challenges by referencing the parents' reactions. This emotional feedback system promotes neural growth and allows the child to safely and securely explore the world. Children with ASD may have neurological vulnerabilities that prevent them from providing parents with the emotional reactions that tell the parents when to introduce a new skill or experience. Without the opportunity for shared emotional experiences with parents, individuals with ASD may not develop dynamic intelligence, a key component in forming social relationships and flexibly adapting to changing environments. Consequently, these children process information in a static and rigid way, leading to difficulties with social relationships, a need for routines and rituals, and problems with transitions.

RDI's main focus is to rebuild the GPR by teaching parents methods to gradually and deliberately promote dynamic intelligence in their child. By teaching children to attend to parental reactions, to share emotions and to use experience-sharing language, a GPR will supposedly be re-established and the individual with ASD will be better able to interact in social situations. RDI does not specify an age at which this intervention should be started or when it is most effective. This intervention focuses on improving six levels outlined to meet the specific needs of the individual and that focus on improving these specific areas of functioning.[1] The six levels are as follows:

- **Emotional Referencing:** learning to evaluate a situation by referencing the other person's emotional expressions.

- **Social Coordination:** participating in collaborative relationships by observing, adapting and regulating one's behavior.

- **Declarative Language:** using language, verbal or nonverbal, to encourage others to interact and share some aspect of one's experience. (This is different from the language most commonly used by individuals with ASD, imperative language, which is geared toward satisfying one's own needs.)

- **Flexible Thinking:** being able to rapidly adapt to one's environment and change cognitive strategies.

- **Relational Information Processing:** solving problems based upon the larger context (i.e., where there may be no right or wrong solutions).

- **Foresight and Hindsight:** thinking about past experiences in a meaningful way to predict or expect potential future events.

Parents are first paired with a local RDI consultant who assesses the level of the parent-child GPR and the child's developmental level using the Relationship Development Assessment (RDA). Trained RDI consultants are listed on the RDI website (www.rdiconnect.com), and parents can choose a consultant based on the services offered in their area. According to the RDA Connect website, consultants certified to conduct RDAs are currently offered in 35 states in the United States and in many countries elsewhere in the world.

After the initial assessment, caregivers meet with their consultant weekly or biweekly to set goals, plan programs and assess progress. Consultants teach parents activities to help their children progress through the levels and stages of the program. When children are ready, each is matched with another local child with ASD so that they can learn to form and maintain relationships in different groups and settings. In addition to meeting with the consultant regularly, parents are encouraged to attend workshops to learn more about the program and meet other parents invested in RDI. Every six months, both the parent and child are re-evaluated using the RDA. The child is monitored for improvements in the six areas outlined above and interventions are modified accordingly.

RDI consultants are extensively trained through an 18-month Certification Training Program. In addition to participating in seminars, lectures and other assignments, consultant-trainees are paired with senior RDI consultants to receive training, feedback and supervision while they work with their first families. Because individuals with a range of educational backgrounds and experience levels could apply to become an RDI consultant, you should shop around to ensure you are comfortable with the RDI consultant's background and experiences before committing to the intervention.

WHAT WILL YOU READ ON THE INTERNET ABOUT RELATIONSHIP DEVELOPMENT INTERVENTION AS A TREATMENT FOR ASD?

Although RDI is a relatively new treatment, there is a lot of information, excitement and hype present in the media. The official website for RDI (www.rdiconnect.com) provides detailed information about the theory behind the program, the program objectives, how to find a consultant and an online store. This website does not provide practical information that parents might seek, such as examples of activities that they could implement, the cost of the program or the recommended length of the program.

There are numerous anecdotal claims about RDI's effectiveness online. The official RDI website claims: "We have found that the RDI Program dramatically increased children's motivation to communicate and use reciprocal language." Many other websites and blogs claim that RDI has been "life-changing" and "extremely successful for all autistic children." However, there is limited research to support this claim.

WHAT DO SCIENTISTS SAY ABOUT RELATIONSHIP DEVELOPMENT INTERVENTION?

RDI emerged from practitioners' experiences with families who have children with ASD and a review of research in the areas of neurology and developmental psychology. Inferred from this research is that a dysfunction in neural systems in the brain leads children with ASD to not engage in these early feedback systems with parents.[2, 3] Thus far no studies have documented a causal link between impairment in early parent-child feedback systems and difficulties in cognitive-development areas in childhood.

There is only one published study of RDI's effectiveness. Dr. Gutstein (the founder of the intervention) and his colleagues examined the effectiveness of RDI for 16 children diagnosed with high functioning ASD.[4] The children were 18 months to eight years of age and had IQ scores in the range 70–118. The researchers claimed that after three years in the program, children showed significant increases in reciprocal communication and social interaction, experience-sharing, and flexible and adaptive behavior as measured by the RDA. Additionally, the results indicated a change in diagnostic category as measured on the Autism Diagnostic Observation Schedule (ADOS) and Autism Diagnostic Interview—Revised (ADI-R). Before treatment, ten children received an "autism" rating and two received an "autism spectrum" rating. After treatment, six children received an "autism spectrum" rating, ten children received a "non-autism" rating, and no children were placed in the "autism" category. (Note that before treatment, the authors were only able to test 12 of the 16 children using the ADOS measure; however, after treatment, they were able to test all 16 of the children.) This indicates that long-term RDI programs might be an effective method in increasing socio-emotional functioning in a sample of high functioning children with ASD.[4] The findings are encouraging and provide a base from which future studies should build. However, due to the researchers' conflict of interest and the lack of control and comparison groups, the findings from this single study are preliminary at best. The National Autism Center's National Standards Project places RDI together with other developmental relationship-based treatments and classifies this category as "emerging treatments" for ASD.[5]

WHAT ARE THE COSTS OF RELATIONSHIP DEVELOPMENT INTERVENTION?

The financial costs of RDI vary depending on the consultant; consultants set their own fees for the components involved in a standard RDI treatment. One consultant advertised the basic program to cost approximately $5000 per year. This does not, however, include costs accrued by attending the "strongly encouraged" parent workshops. The workshop training ranges in price from $250–300 for a two-day seminar to $2000 for a four-day seminar, plus travel expenses. Overall, the financial costs could add up to around $7000 for the first year of RDI treatment. Since families often remain in the RDI program for three years or more, the lowest estimated cost for this time commitment would be approximately $21,000. Insurance companies rarely cover this treatment.

Time commitments are often costly as well. Beyond the initial assessment and the workshops, parents and children generally spend about three hours a day on activities and objectives. Parents also meet with the consultant twice a month to review videos of their child, and to discuss goals and strategies.

RELATIONSHIP DEVELOPMENT INTERVENTION (RDI)

Ages	→	all ages		
Anecdotal parental support	→	not much	mixed	positive
Scientific evidence	→	weak	moderate	strong
Availability	→	limited	moderate	wide
Cost (time and money)	→	minimal	moderate	high

15
SENSORY INTEGRATION THERAPY

Elisabeth Hollister Sandberg
and Susan E. Michelson

WHAT IS SENSORY INTEGRATION THERAPY?

Sensory Integration therapy (SI therapy) is a treatment for ASD and various other conditions based upon the assumption that the child's brain has difficulty processing input from the sensory systems. The tactile (touch), vestibular (balance) and proprioceptive (physical coordination and awareness) systems seem to be the most dominantly affected. SI therapy stimulates and challenges a child's senses in a controlled manner. Over time, this is thought to improve the brain's ability to process sensory information, which in turn reduces problem behaviors that result from sensory overloads. SI therapy is most commonly used as a therapy for young children, and is used to treat a variety of developmental challenges, not only ASD.

HOW DOES SENSORY INTEGRATION THERAPY SUPPOSEDLY WORK AS A TREATMENT FOR ASD?

SI therapy is an occupational therapy that addresses problems with sensory processing regulation by stimulating and challenging the senses in gradual and regulated ways. Through SI therapy, children become better able to handle sensory input and regulate their corresponding arousal, attention, emotions and behaviors. Anna Jean Ayres, an occupational therapist, developed the rationale for SI therapy in the early 1970s.[1] According to her theory, the body naturally processes and integrates information received from all of the senses using areas of the brain responsible for attention, arousal and emotion. When the body receives sensory information that it cannot process, the result is akin to a "traffic jam" that produces maladaptive emotional and behavioral responses.

Children with difficulty processing sensory information may be either over- or under-responsive to input from one or more of the senses—sights, sounds, tastes or smells. For example, a child may be overwhelmed by a visually "busy" environment or may strongly dislike flashing lights; or a child may be especially sensitive to loud noises or unexpected noises, such as sirens or alarms. Reactions to improper processing of sensation can result in avoidant or escape behaviors (closing eyes, clasping hands over ears) or excessive sensation-seeking behaviors (touching too roughly, talking too loudly). According to the theory, dysfunctional sensory processing may also manifest itself as distractibility, physical clumsiness, impulsivity, transition problems, the inability to calm down, poor self-concept, or delays in speech, language, motor skills or academic achievement. In using SI therapy for ASD, it is assumed that some of these common symptoms of ASD can be alleviated by addressing problems in sensory processing regulation.

SI therapy emphasizes four basic principles:[2]

- **Just Right Challenge:** SI therapy fosters the child's ability to successfully meet sensory challenges through play activities.

- **Adaptive Response:** SI therapy promotes adaptation to challenges using new, effective strategies.

- **Active Engagement:** SI activities are specifically designed to be fun and engaging.

- **Child Directed:** SI therapy facilitates a child's "buy in" through activities tailored to the interests of the child.

During a typical SI therapy session, activities are presented to stimulate the target sensory systems and promote the development of adaptive responses. For example, disruptions to the tactile system (related to sensory experiences involving pain, temperature and pressure) may produce signs of withdrawal from touch (refusal to wear certain fabrics, dislike of having hair or face washed, avoidance of getting hands dirty) or may result in efforts to seek additional stimulation (touching others or fiddling with objects). To address these issues, an SI treatment plan might focus on tactile activities involving a variety of sensations and textures such as water play, skin brushing, manipulation of dough and sand play. These activities provide opportunities for children to experience these stimulations in positive and supported ways. The goal is for the child to learn adaptive ways of responding to the stimulation and to generalize those responses to other situations and environments.

Children who have problems with sensory processing regulation are sometimes referred to as having "sensory integration dysfunction." This designation is not an official diagnosis recognized by either the American Psychiatric Association or the World Health Organization due to the fact that the symptoms for sensory integration dysfunction are shared with a number of other disorders, including ASD, attention deficit hyperactivity disorder, depression, anxiety and learning disabilities. The approach to treatment, however, is the same regardless of a child's diagnosis.

WHAT WILL YOU READ ON THE INTERNET ABOUT SENSORY INTEGRATION THERAPY AS A TREATMENT FOR ASD?

SI therapy is a very popular form of therapy for young children with ASD. Websites specifically devoted to SI therapy typically explain the nature of sensory integration problems, what the common symptoms are, and the range of attention, emotional and behavioral problems that may be affected.

The individualized treatment approach of SI therapy is appealing to parents of children with unique sensory sensitivities. Most of the well-known ASD websites include information about sensory dysfunction and how SI therapy may decrease children's emotional and behavioral problems. Testimonials suggest that using SI therapy to reduce children's sensory issues increases their social responsiveness, attention and language production. SI therapy has reportedly been "transformative" for some children with ASD. There are many accounts of children who could not tolerate being bathed, who would not wear shoes, or who gagged on foods with certain textures overcoming those difficulties through SI therapy. Only a few websites consider the scientific evidence supporting SI therapy, and even fewer present scientifically validated evidence for the use of SI therapy for ASD.

Other online SI therapy resources include quizzes and checklists that help parents determine whether a child has a "sensory processing disorder." Many of these include links to companies that manufacture toys and equipment for children with sensory integration difficulties such as bouncers, pediatric scooter boards and ramps, and swings. These resources are often pitched as being "more appropriate" for children with sensory integration issues than regular toys, though such claims are neither explained nor supported by research studies. Testimonial statements from parents are often included in these advertisements. As discussed below, such equipment can be quite expensive and most websites do not provide information on how to utilize the items for the desired therapeutic effect. There are also many websites that offer tips on devising sensory activities at low or no cost using common household and craft materials.

WHAT DO SCIENTISTS SAY ABOUT SENSORY INTEGRATION THERAPY?

Despite the fact that SI therapy is widely incorporated in early interventions for ASD, there is very little scientific evidence supporting SI therapy as an effective treatment. This is due in part to the fact that Sensory Integration therapy was born in the occupational therapy field, a relatively new field with a stronger focus on service rather than research. Also, because SI therapy typically takes place over a long time period (months to years) during the early years of rapid developmental growth, it is very challenging to scientifically establish whether changes in ASD symptoms are actually the result of the SI therapy or of maturation.

Research on the efficacy of Sensory Integration therapy for the treatment of ASD has yielded mixed results. A review article published in 2000 identified just four outcome studies of SI therapy and found the studies either to contain too few study participants or to be too poorly designed to draw confident conclusions concerning the efficacy of the therapy.[3] A 2005 review of the scientific data available about SI therapy states that approximately half of the studies of Sensory Integration therapy techniques find support for the treatment while the remaining half fail to find improvement compared to other treatment approaches.[2] Research studies that compare SI therapy to other treatments in carefully controlled settings are rare.

More recently, in 2011, researchers compared the effectiveness of SI therapy to a fine-motor treatment for a sample of 37 children 6–12 years of age with ASD.[4] Pretests and posttests were used to measure motor skills, sensory processing and social factors. Therapeutic goals were set for each child. After receiving several treatment sessions per week over a six-week period, it was found that the SI therapy group had made better progress toward attaining therapeutic goals and showed decreased ASD mannerisms, but that social skill improvement did not vary between the groups.

A new study launched in 2010 at Vanderbilt University compares SI therapy to a language acquisition technique in a group of 40 children with ASD. This study is unique in that the researchers will examine not only changes in behavior and social performance, but also changes in brain waves. This will allow the researchers to examine directly whether SI therapy changes sensory processes in the brain, and whether it does so more effectively than other common treatment approaches. This study was still underway at the time of this book's publication.

The National Autism Center's National Standards Project in 2009 classified SI therapy as an "unestablished treatment"—one for which there is little to no evidence in support of its effectiveness.[5] The American Academy of

Pediatrics states that "Occupational therapy using sensory integration techniques to address sensory processing problems is commonly used in children with ASD."[6] Although many believe occupational therapy is subjectively effective in educational and clinical settings, research data to support its effectiveness are scant.

WHAT ARE THE COSTS OF SENSORY INTEGRATION THERAPY?

SI therapy can be implemented as either an individual or a group treatment. Group sessions range from $30 to $100 per hour, with individual sessions generally costing close to $100 per hour.[7] Because SI therapy is a type of occupational therapy, it is often covered by insurance when prescribed or ordered by a physician. Schools may offer occupational therapy services to qualifying children at no cost, though the availability of those services is likely to vary based upon geographic location and local educational resources.

The length of treatment is individualized by need. Typically, children need at least a few months of SI therapy, usually two or three times per week, before any improvements might be observed. Continual reinforcement of sensory activities is an essential element to the treatment, so parents must be willing and able to learn, practice and apply the sensory activities at home.

Parents have the option of purchasing the equipment utilized by licensed occupational therapists, such as items for suspension, vestibular stimulation, and weight and resistance exercises. This equipment can be quite expensive and most websites do not provide information on how to utilize the items for the desired therapeutic effect. Consultation with a licensed occupational therapist about home equipment is essential.

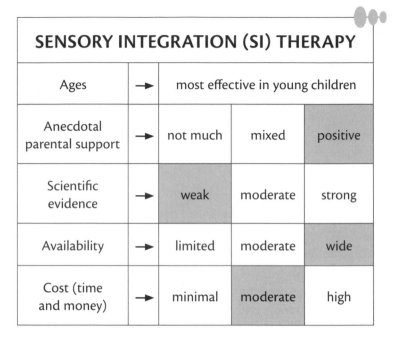

SENSORY INTEGRATION (SI) THERAPY			
Ages	→ most effective in young children		
Anecdotal parental support	→ not much	mixed	positive
Scientific evidence	→ weak	moderate	strong
Availability	→ limited	moderate	wide
Cost (time and money)	→ minimal	moderate	high

16

THE SON-RISE PROGRAM

Joseph C. Viola and
Elisabeth Hollister Sandberg

WHAT IS THE SON-RISE PROGRAM?

The Son-Rise Program is a comprehensive treatment and education program for families of children with ASD. It is affiliated exclusively with the Autism Treatment Center of America.[1] Founded in 1974 by Barry and Samahria Kaufman, the Son-Rise Program trains parents to join in behaviors with their ASD child, rather than attempting to modify or stop them. Accepting a child's behavior, rather than attempting to change it, promotes an environment of safety in which connections and rapport can be built. The Son-Rise Program takes place exclusively in the home between caregivers and the child.[2, 3]

HOW DOES THE SON-RISE PROGRAM SUPPOSEDLY WORK AS A TREATMENT FOR ASD?

The Son-Rise Program was built upon the successful experience of the Kaufman family raising their son, Raun, who was believed to be severely autistic as a young child. Although Raun was nonverbal and unengaged, the Kaufman family spurned the popular behavioral ASD interventions of the 1970s in favor of a more relational approach, one grounded in acceptance rather than disapproval of certain behaviors. After their intensive efforts, Raun grew up to be an intelligent, articulate, successful adult.

At the heart of the Son-Rise Program is ensuring safety and trust—not judging behaviors as good or bad, and not insisting upon certain behaviors. The Son-Rise Program is guided by principles grounded in an attitude of acceptance, not disapproval, and is concerned first and foremost with helping ASD children learn how to sustain relationships in their lives. The Son-Rise Program maintains that ASD is a relational disorder and that participating fully with ASD children in a manner consistent with their natural behaviors is the best way to facilitate development. Prescriptive behavioral programs such as Applied Behavioral Analysis are seen as implicitly labeling the child as "bad" in ways that undermine parent-child rapport and limit the likelihood that a child with ASD will want to relate to the parent. This is believed to inhibit rather than promote social development.

Parents play the most critical role in the program. The Son-Rise Program challenges parents to adopt a holistic, relationship-based approach to supporting their ASD child. Parents are asked to go beyond simply learning corrective behavioral strategies to developing and embracing an attitude of acceptance about their child's relational difficulties. In the same way that a new parent engages supportively with a newborn infant (understanding that they must go to the infant's crib, use baby language and make faces to create an interaction, and find ways to relate using the baby's own systems of communicating), the Son-Rise Program asks parents to find ways to similarly connect with, bond and understand their child with ASD.

The Son-Rise Program educates and trains parents in three important techniques: creating a distraction-free setting, using behavior to build a bond, and increasing/ maintaining eye contact.

Creating a distraction-free setting

The Son-Rise Program asserts that in order for development to occur, an optimal learning environment must be created. Emphasis is placed upon creating a home environment in which the parent reduces environmental distractions that compete for the child's attention, thereby maximizing the child's ability to enjoy the parental relationship. The program assumes that most children with ASD suffer from sensory overload. Parents must create a space in their home that allows a child to focus exclusively on the parents. Creating an optimal environment for parent-child interactions is believed to enhance the child's experiences in social relationships and to increase the child's desire and ability to relate with others. The Son-Rise Program offers practical suggestions for optimizing the environment (neutral paint colors, natural or incandescent lighting, a floor free of all objects, etc.). Once established, this special room will be the place where the child spends most of his or her time; others will come to this space to interact with the child.

Using behavior to build a bond (to "join" a child)

In contrast to other treatments for ASD that work to stop children's undesirable behaviors and replace them with more socially appropriate ones, the Son-Rise Program views a child's behavior as a doorway through which parents can enter a relationship with that child. Parents are encouraged to view the child's behavior as part of the whole child. "Joining" children in their behavior is the centerpiece of the Son-Rise Program. Joining begins with a period of observation during which the parent simply observes the child's behavior. After a period of observation, the parent enters the child's space—sitting two to three feet away—and mimics exactly what the child is doing. Parents are encouraged to join in whatever game the child is playing and synchronize their actions to match the rhythm and pace of both the verbal and nonverbal components of the child's behaviors. Done with sincerity, joining is believed to offer a way of connecting with the child using his or her own language. It communicates to the child that the parent cares for and wants to be close to the child, offering respect for and acceptance of the child's behavior.

Increasing/maintaining eye contact

A third element that the Son-Rise Program focuses on is one of the more fundamental elements of social interaction: eye contact. Successful connections with others convey warmth and acceptance through eye contact, facial expressions, tone of voice and other nonverbal subtleties of communication. Ultimately, the Son-Rise Program strives to make eye contact a primary way of expressing the desire to connect with another person. The goal is to build genuine eye contact into every encounter with the child. Skills for making meaningful eye contact are modeled by parents in their interactions with their children. Parents are trained to position themselves such that it is easy for a child to look at them (e.g., in front of the child, at eye level, two to three feet away, putting a desired object directly in front of their eyes). Parents are also trained to celebrate every time the child seeks to connect through eye contact (cheering, throwing arms in the air, dancing), in order to further enhance this aspect of the social connection.

WHAT WILL YOU READ ON THE INTERNET ABOUT THE SON-RISE PROGRAM AS A TREATMENT FOR ASD?

Most searches will yield direct links to the Son-Rise Program's official materials (as well as to its closely linked training facility called the Option Program). Promotional websites offer bold statements of success, along with many compelling parental testimonials. Supporters say that through the Son-Rise Program children with ASD can become affectionate, communicative, non-aggressive, sharing, socially engaged individuals.

A more extensive search is required to tap into websites focusing on the controversies. Skeptics of the Son-Rise Program reference the "cult-like" nature of the program's supporters. Arguments are made about the practical impossibility of creating the optimal therapeutic environment while living in the real world. Some question whether the "recovery" of the child (Raun) upon which the entire program is based was indeed a recovery from severe or even moderate autism. These critics suggest that Raun may have been primarily a speech-delayed preschooler who, at best, fell on the high functioning end of the autism spectrum. This raises speculation about his "miraculous" progress.

WHAT DO SCIENTISTS SAY ABOUT THE SON-RISE PROGRAM?

The Son-Rise Program has distanced itself from more behavioral interventions that treat ASD. The exclusive focus on the relational elements of ASD treatment poses a challenge for those seeking to measure the efficacy of the program. The Son-Rise Program embraces all ASD behaviors, desirable or not, and asks parents to join in the behaviors with the child, accepting these behaviors as part of the child's natural way of being. Virtually all other ASD treatments see behavior as a specific element to be changed, and the effectiveness of those interventions is measured by looking at changes in specific behaviors. The preferred unit of analysis in the Son-Rise Program is the whole child (as a collection of thoughts, feelings and behaviors), something for which there is no measurement tool. As a result, there are no studies yet within the scientific community indicating that the Son-Rise Program is effective.

The absence of scientific support surrounding the Son-Rise Program is not surprising, given the ways in which the program's founders fought against the behavioral tide of ASD treatment of the 1970s. The Son-Rise Program, in many ways, was created to represent the opposite of behavioral modification programs targeting measureable behaviors. In 2006 the Autism Treatment Center of America initiated a long-term research initiative with two universities to scientifically investigate the effectiveness of the Son-Rise Program. Results are not yet available.

Although the Son-Rise Program has become a popular training program for parents of ASD children, it remains an outlier in the scientific community. The National Autism Center's National Standards Project did not include the Son-Rise Program in its analysis in 2009 because there is no evidence upon which to evaluate its effectiveness.[4]

WHAT ARE THE COSTS OF THE SON-RISE PROGRAM?

There are different treatment options within the Son-Rise Program, each of which includes activities, social collaborations, support services (books, movies) and advanced individual support. The only required cost is that of a five-day group training program for parents involving peer support groups, education about ASD and breakout sessions led by Son-Rise experts. The cost is approximately $2200 per parent for the five-day exercise, plus travel expenses. There are supplemental books and instructional DVDs available for purchase.

The time investment required for the full-time Son-Rise Program is considerable. Anecdotal reports of children with remarkable recoveries typically report one-on-one therapy for 40–70 hours per week for two to three years before the age of six. Such an effort is probably not compatible with parental employment, and care must be arranged for siblings (parents are encouraged to recruit family and friends as volunteers to help with the effort). There are part-time (10–30 hours per week) and "lifestyle" (30 minutes per day) program options for families who cannot commit to the full-time program. These are options that allow families to try some of the Son-Rise techniques before (or in lieu of) committing to a dedicated full-time program. Presumably the claims of progress are more moderate for these programs.

SON-RISE PROGRAM

Ages	→	all ages		
Anecdotal parental support	→	not much	mixed	positive
Scientific evidence	→	weak	moderate	strong
Availability	→	limited	moderate	wide
Cost (time and money)	→	minimal	moderate	high

17

TEACCH (TREATMENT AND EDUCATION OF AUTISTIC AND RELATED COMMUNICATION-HANDICAPPED CHILDREN)

Mary Beth McCullough and
Elisabeth Hollister Sandberg

WHAT IS TEACCH?

Developed in 1971 at the University of North Carolina (UNC), TEACCH (Treatment and Education of Autistic and Related Communication-Handicapped Children) is an intervention program that focuses on modifying environments, materials and presentation methods in ways that reflect the specific learning styles of children with ASD. TEACCH is unique in that it provides services to individuals of all ages and skill levels with ASD, and can be applied in numerous settings. By building on the existing skills, needs and interests of a person with ASD, the goal is to promote "meaning and independence" through "flexible and individualized" support to ASD individuals and their families.[1] Teaching strategies include providing directions using minimal language, offering clear and timely prompts, and giving external reinforcement. A defining feature of TEACCH is the creation of a highly structured learning environment within which intensive intervention can occur.

HOW DOES TEACCH SUPPOSEDLY WORK AS A TREATMENT FOR ASD?

TEACCH activities focus on teaching individuals within a "Culture of Autism" framework—embracing rather than rejecting the distinct patterns of thinking and communication seen in individuals with ASD in order to assist them in better understanding their environment. Individuals with ASD process visual information well and have a keen eye for detail, yet have difficulties in areas such as receptive and expressive language, organizing details into a coherent whole, coping with changes in the environment and sequential memory. With these strengths and challenges in mind, TEACCH uses an intervention technique called Structured Teaching to best meet ASD learning needs. Structured Teaching not only takes the ASD learning style into account, but also focuses on the individual's specific strengths and challenges. Individualized person- and family-centered plans are developed for each client to focus on his or her unique learning needs and goals.[2]

The four main elements of Structured Teaching are physical structure, scheduling, work systems and task organization:

- **Physical structure** refers to clear physical boundaries in the individual's environment that indicate distinct areas or zones (work, play, music, snack). The physical layout of the environment is structured in a way to minimize visual and auditory distractions (e.g., using natural lighting, neutral classroom colors). Visual cues assist individuals in organizing, clarifying and understanding their environment and what is expected in certain activities. For example, the use of colored containers can assist the individual in sorting colored materials into different groups.

- **Scheduling** refers to providing the individual with a schedule or planner that clearly indicates the daily, weekly and monthly activities through words or pictures. For very young children this might take the form of a strip of ordered pictures representing activities. Concrete scheduling helps individuals with difficulties with sequential memory and organization to understand what they are supposed to be doing at a certain time as well as the sequence of events. This can allow for smoother transitions from one activity to the next, and minimizes anxiety about upcoming events.

- **Work systems** indicate what tasks individuals are supposed to do, how much there is to be done, and how they will know when they are finished. The goal is to organize the work system in such a way that the individual will be able to work independently on tasks. For example, work tasks for specific skills are physically displayed in baskets with the work to be completed on the student's left. The exact task and amount of work are clearly defined on the baskets. The student completes tasks independently and places the finished work in a basket to his or her right. After the task is complete, the student can refer to his or her schedule to determine the next activity.

- **Task organization** gives a representation of each task in the work system, including step-by-step visual instructions on how to complete the task, and what the task looks like when complete.

All of these elements described above encourage individuals to develop a routine that involves checking one's schedule and following the work system in place each day. These are critical skills that foster autonomy in multiple settings throughout a person's lifetime.[2]

WHAT WILL YOU READ ON THE INTERNET ABOUT TEACCH AS A TREATMENT FOR ASD?

TEACCH is a popular and accessible topic on the internet. The official website "Division TEACCH" from the UNC School of Medicine (www.teacch.com) provides a very thorough and detailed introduction into the technique. It is mainly written for parents trying to find services for their child in North Carolina. Numerous other websites provide information about programs outside of North Carolina. There is widespread acceptance among parents and teachers about the need for consistent structure when working with children with ASD. Although official program websites explain the general ways in which TEACCH provides this structure, it is difficult to find details about specific work systems or tasks that one can implement without purchasing TEACCH equipment through the official website.

Critics raise concerns about TEACCH being a rigid behavior management system suitable for use only in dedicated special education classrooms.[3] Some argue that TEACCH programs have low expectations (being able to follow a schedule and complete very basic tasks) and that it works only with low functioning individuals with ASD who need this sort of remedial training and who cannot engage with their environments in more sophisticated and complicated ways. Some claim that TEACCH is practical only for younger children who are not expected to work or function in many different settings every day. They argue that TEACCH is not useful for higher functioning children who integrate into mainstream classrooms because of the structure "capsule" that is required.

WHAT DO SCIENTISTS SAY ABOUT TEACCH?

The various components of the ASD profile (the Culture of Autism) upon which TEACCH is built have a great deal of scientific support. In other words, the foundational skills that TEACCH addresses have been clearly established as being areas of challenge for individuals with ASD.[4] Specifically, research has shown that individuals with ASD have:

- relative strength in, and preference for, processing visual information (compared to difficulties with auditory processing, particularly of language)

- heightened attention to details, but difficulty with sequencing, integrating, connecting or deriving meaning from them

- enormous variability in attention (individuals can be very distractible at times, and at other times intensely focused, with difficulties shifting attention efficiently)

- communication problems, which vary by developmental level, but always include impairments in the initiation and social use of language (pragmatics)

- difficulty with concepts of time including moving through activities too quickly or too slowly and having problems recognizing the beginning or end of an activity, how long the activity will last, and when it will be finished

- tendency to become attached to routines and the settings where they are established, so that activities may be difficult to transfer or generalize from the original learning situation, and disruptions in routines can be uncomfortable, confusing or upsetting

- very intense interests and impulses to engage in favored activities and difficulties disengaging once engaged

- marked sensory preferences and aversions.[4]

Research examining the effectiveness of TEACCH as an intervention for ASD has been ongoing since the mid-1970s. In 2010 researchers conducted a review of nine published studies to examine the impact of TEACCH across a wide range of skills, functioning levels and ages (2–50 years).[4] Although early studies did not meet currently accepted standards for scientific rigor, the converging evidence suggests that TEACCH may be effective in improving nonverbal communication skills and independent task completion.[5] Additional evidence suggests that TEACCH also plays a role in decreasing restricted, repetitive and stereotyped patterns of behavior in individuals over time.[6] These results have been observed in the short and long term, and across settings (home, inclusive and special education classrooms, and the workplace). Discrepancies have emerged regarding TEACCH's impact on the areas of functional communication and social interaction skills. While some studies show notable increases in these areas, others show no gains.[7]

Keep in mind that all of the studies about the effectiveness of TEACCH had limitations in study design and methodology that potentially affect the validity and generalizability of the results. First, the TEACCH strategies have been evolving since the early 1970s. Data from early studies cannot be expected to be reliably consistent with more recent data because the interventions were really not the same. Study sample sizes were often small (ranging from 1 to 34 individuals) and only about half of the studies compared the TEACCH approach with another method. Second, the studies have not been blind; raters of outcomes knew which individuals had participated in TEACCH and which had not. Third, the objectivity of some of the researchers may have been compromised because of their involvement in the development or implementation of the TEACCH program—a conflict of interest. Finally, a critical problem in TEACCH research is the philosophy of the TEACCH program itself. Because TEACCH relies on individualizing treatments to children and adults, different techniques are applied to each person, making it difficult to research and generalize.

Overall, scientific evidence suggests that TEACCH may be an effective method for individuals from two to 50 years with ASD in improving specific behaviors, such as use of nonverbal communication, social reciprocity and functional independence, as well as decreasing repetitive behaviors. Due to conflicting evidence, however, TEACCH's effect on communication and social interaction skills is still unclear, and rigorous studies comparing TEACCH with other interventions are lacking.

The National Autism Center's National Standards Project includes TEACCH under "Structured Teaching"—classified as an "emerging treatment" for ASD.[8]

WHAT ARE THE COSTS OF TEACCH?

The financial and time commitments for TEACCH programs are highly dependent on which service or program is used. There are currently nine regional TEACCH Centers in North Carolina; these school-based programs are free of charge to qualifying residents of the state. School-based programs in North Carolina often implement TEACCH methods seven hours a day, five days a week. Elsewhere in the United States, trained therapists and parents use TEACCH methods within other settings. Parents can learn to implement basic TEACCH strategies at home by attending TEACCH workshops, which are mostly offered in North Carolina at a cost of $130–200 for a one-day workshop, plus travel expenses. Parents can purchase books and DVDs from the TEACCH website that range in cost from $12 to $95. The time commitment required to set up a home-based TEACCH program (making visual schedules, reorganizing certain rooms for physical structure, setting up work systems and task organization schedules) can be significant. Implementation of the program, once set up, generally consumes several hours per day.

TEACCH (TREATMENT AND EDUCATION OF AUTISTIC AND RELATED COMMUNICATION-HANDICAPPED CHILDREN)

Ages	→	all ages		
Anecdotal parental support	→	not much	mixed	positive
Scientific evidence	→	weak	moderate	strong
Availability	→	limited	moderate	wide
Cost (time and money)	→	minimal	moderate	high

18

A NOTE ABOUT MEDICATIONS

Elisabeth Hollister Sandberg
and Becky L. Spritz

By "medications" we are referring to psychopharmacological agents that are specifically prescribed by physicians to manage the symptoms of ASD. We do not use the term to refer to dietary supplements (which have been covered in Chapter 8) or to standard over-the-counter remedies that one might electively take to treat a headache or a cough.

We have not included medications as a treatment chapter in this book for two main reasons: first and foremost, using medication is not a decision that parents are empowered to make on their own; second, there is no drug that directly treats the underlying causes of ASD. Instead, medications are used to address troublesome symptoms of the disorder. Medication regimens are deeply entangled with the co-morbid disorders of ASD (depression, anxiety, ADHD). Decision-making about medication gets extremely complicated very quickly, and the scientific outcome data cannot be easily distilled. Given this, we believe that discussions of the potential risks and benefits of medications are best left between the parents and prescribing professionals with whom a trusting relationship has been established.

If, as a parent, you are uncomfortable with a doctor's recommendations about medicating your child, you are well within your rights to request a second opinion. Unlike using medications to manage a well-understood medical condition (such as diabetes or high blood pressure), medicating children for the behavioral symptoms of ASD is not straightforward. It is as much of an art as it is a science. And, unlike conditions such as diabetes, with ASD there is no edict that you must medicate. Sometimes decisions about medications are clear, in instances of severe self-injurious behavior for example. More often, though, the decisions boil down to quality of life questions with uncertain outcomes. Families and physicians rely on medications to control symptoms and behaviors that are unmanageable through behavioral interventions or that are interfering with a child's ability to participate in other therapeutic interventions. Use of medications is fairly common in older children and adolescents with ASD, and in some instances physicians will recommend medications for children as young as three years.

Because medications feature prominently—and typically beneficially—in the lives of many families dealing with ASD, we have compiled a list of the medications that are frequently prescribed to children with ASD so that you can at least know what they are and how they are commonly used. The generic names of medications are in regular type, while *brand names are in italics.* The FDA has approved only two drugs specifically for use in people with ASD: risperidone/ *Risperdal* and aripiprazole/*Abilify.* Both of these drugs, which have very similar actions, address specific symptom patterns found in some (not all!) children with ASD. In addition to these two officially approved medications, however, there are many other drugs used to mitigate the symptom profile of ASD and the other disorders that occur with it. Most of these medications fall into one of four basic categories:

- **Stimulants:** these drugs are used to improve attention and reduce impulsivity and hyperactivity for children with ADHD as well as many other disorders for which impulsive and/or hyperactive behavior are symptoms.

- **Antidepressants/anxiolytics:** these drugs are used to treat depression, aggression, tantrums, irritability, repetitive behaviors and anxiety. Note that most drugs officially labeled antidepressants are also effective for treating anxiety.

- **Antipsychotics:** these drugs are used to reduce repetitive behaviors, self-injurious behaviors, withdrawal and aggression. Although they are called antipsychotics, these drugs are almost never used to treat actual psychosis in children with ASD.

- **Mood stabilizers:** these drugs are used to regulate intense mood shifts.

Don't get caught up in the category names—"stimulants" are not necessarily stimulating, and an "antipsychotic" may sound like an extreme and inappropriate treatment for a child with ASD! The category names are carried over from other disciplines where the drugs were initially characterized, and still help doctors and other providers to organize the drugs when thinking about medication therapy.

Although there are only two FDA-approved drugs specifically for treating symptoms of ASD, there are many others that can be useful. The regulation of drugs in the United States requires that a medication show efficacy to treat a specific condition (in other words, to have a specific indication). The approval process is expensive, so manufacturers usually pick one major indication and obtain approval to treat that one condition. However, most drugs can treat many conditions. To account for this, physicians' licenses specifically allow them to prescribe "off label"— using their professional expertise and judgment about how a particular medicine might be of benefit to a particular child. Here, the term "off label" means the physician is prescribing the drug for a condition not addressed by the manufacturer's application to have the drug approved, but a condition for which the drug is known or believed to be useful by the community of physicians. Two things are notable here: first, most medications in the United States are prescribed off label, and second, the medication treatment of ASD is changing rapidly as physicians and researchers work to find the best ways to use medications to help manage symptoms and improve treatment.

Prescription medications for children with ASD are almost always managed by a specialist (a psychiatrist or a psychopharmacologist) rather than a general pediatrician. Parents should never, ever, "try out" a medication that has not been specifically prescribed for their child. Physicians typically work with parents to find a combination of medications that best addresses the symptoms that need to be controlled for a particular child. Children with ASD are constantly growing and developing—both physically (they get bigger, so they need more medication to achieve the same effect, and their bodies metabolize drugs differently as they develop) and psychologically (different symptoms become more or less prominent over time). Thus, parents should expect medications to be a constantly moving target. This is not a bad thing. Quite the contrary—the child's changing medication requirements over time indicate dynamic development. Medications come and go, both in any child's specific regimen and in the realm of what is available.

We have organized the list below alphabetically by brand name to facilitate future research on a particular medication and its effects. This list is not exhaustive, but should cover most of those commonly prescribed for ASD.

Abilify [aripiprazole]	Antipsychotic
Adderall [amphetamine]	Stimulant
Anafranil [clomipramine]	Antidepressant
BuSpar [buspirone]	Anxiolytic
Celexa [citalopram]	Antidepressant
Cibalith-S [lithium citrate]	Mood stabilizer
Clozaril [clozapine]	Antipsychotic
Concerta [methylphenidate (long acting)]	Stimulant
Cymbalta [duloxetine]	Antidepressant
Depakote [valproic acid]	Mood stabilizer
Dexedrine [dextroamphetamine]	Stimulant
Dextrostat [dextroamphetamine]	Stimulant
Effexor [venlafaxine]	Antidepressant
Elavil [amitriptyline]	Antidepressant
Eskalith [lithium carbonate]	Mood stabilizer
Focalin [dexmethylphenidate]	Stimulant
Intunive [guanfacine]	Nonstimulant with stimulant-like effects
Haldol [haloperidol]	Antipsychotic
Lexapro [escitalopram]	Antidepressant
Lithobid [lithium carbonate]	Mood stabilizer
Luvox [fluvoxamine]	Antidepressant
Mellaril [thioridazine]	Antipsychotic
Metadate ER [methylphenidate (extended release)]	Stimulant
Orap [pimozide]	Antipsychotic
Paxil [paroxetine]	Antidepressant
Prozac [fluoxetine]	Antidepressant
Risperdal [risperidone]	Antipsychotic
Ritalin [methylphenidate]	Stimulant
Seroquel [quetiapine]	Antipsychotic
Serzone [nefazodone]	Antidepressant
Sinequan [doxepin]	Antidepressant

Strattera [atomoxetine]	Nonstimulant with stimulant-like effects
Tegretol [carbamazepine]	Mood stabilizer
Tenex [guanfacine]	Nonstimulant with stimulant-like effects
Tofranil [imipramine]	Antidepressant
Vyvanase [lisdexamfetamine]	Stimulant
Wellbutrin [bupropion]	Antidepressant
Zoloft [sertraline]	Antidepressant
Zyprexa [olanzapine]	Antipsychotic

References

3. APPLIED BEHAVIORAL ANALYSIS

1. Landau, E. (2009). Choice autism treatment offers benefits, has limits. *CNN Health*, March 31. Retrieved June 10, 2012, from http://articles.cnn.com/2009-03-31/health/autism.applied.behavior.analysis_1_autism-therapies-elevator-new-trial?_s=PM:HEALTH.

2. Behavior Analyst Certification Board. (n.d.). *Behavior Analyst Certification Board (BACB)*. Retrieved April 24, 2012, from www.bacb.com.

3. Association for Behavior Analysis International. (n.d.). *Association for Behavior Analysis International (ABAI)*. Retrieved April 24, 2012, from www.abainternational.org/index.asp.

4. Lovaas, O. I. (1987). Behavioral treatment and normal educational and intellectual functioning in young autistic children. *Journal of Consulting and Clinical Psychology, 55*(1), 3–9.

5. Reichow, B. (2012). Overview of meta-analyses on early intensive behavioral intervention for young children with autism spectrum disorders. *Journal of Autism and Developmental Disorders, 42*(4), 512–520.

6. United States Surgeon General. (1998). *Mental Health: A Report of the Surgeon General.* Washington, DC: US Surgeon General.

7. American Academy of Pediatrics. (2001). The pediatrician's role in the diagnosis and management of autism spectrum disorders in children. *Pediatrics, 107*(5), 1221–1226.

8. National Autism Center. (2009). *The National Standards Project: Addressing the Need for Evidence Based Practice Guidelines for Autism Spectrum Disorders.* Randolph, MA: National Autism Center.

4. CHELATION

1. University of Maryland Medical Center. (2011). *Ethylenediaminetetraacetic Acid.* Retrieved June 10, 2012, from www.umm.edu/altmed/articles/ethylenediaminetetraacetic-acid-000302.htm.

2. Ip, P., Wong, V., Ho, M., Lee, J., and Wong, W. (2004). Mercury exposure in children with autistic spectrum disorder: Case-control study. *Journal of Child Neurology, 19*, 431–434.

3. Williams, P. G., Hersh, J. H., Allard, A., and Sears, L. L. (2008). A controlled study of mercury levels in hair samples of children with autism as compared to their typically developing siblings. *Research in Autism Spectrum Disorders, 2*(1), 170–175.

4. Institute of Medicine, Immunization Safety Review Committee. (2004). *Immunization Safety Review: Vaccines and Autism.* Washington, DC: National Academies Press.

5. Parker, S. K. (2004). Thimerosal-containing vaccines and autistic spectrum disorder: A critical review of published original data. *Pediatrics, 114*(3), 793–804.

6. Doja, A., and Roberts, W. (2006). Immunizations and autism: A review of the literature. *Canadian Journal of Neurological Sciences, 33*, 341–346.

7. Gerber, J., and Offit, P. (2009). Vaccines and autism: A tale of shifting hypotheses. *Clinical Infectious Diseases, 48*(4), 456–461.

8. Adams, J. B., Baral, M., Geis, E., Mitchell, J., *et al.* (2009). Safety and efficacy of oral DMSA therapy for children with autism spectrum disorders: Part B—Behavioral results. *BMC Clinical Pharmacology, 9*(1), 17.

9. Atwood, K., Woeckner, E., Baratz, R., and Sampson, W. (2008). Why the NIH Trial to Assess Chelation Therapy (TACT) should be abandoned. *Medscape Journal of Medicine, 10*(5), 115.

5. CRANIOSACRAL THERAPY

1. Upledger Institute International (n.d.). *Discover CranioSacral Therapy.* Retrieved June 10, 2012, from http://upledger.com/content.asp?id=26.

2. Green, C., Martin, C., Bassett, K., and Kazanjian, A. (1999). A systematic review of craniosacral therapy: Biological plausibility, assessment reliability and clinical effectiveness. *Complementary Therapies in Medicine, 7*(4), 201–207.

3. Association for Science in Autism Treatment (ASAT). (n.d.). *Craniosacral Therapy.* Retrieved June 10, 2012, from www.asatonline.org/treatment/treatments/craniosacral.htm.

4. Autism-World. (n.d.). *How CranioSacral Therapy (CST) Works for Autism.* Retrieved June 10, 2012, from www.autism-world.com/index.php/2009/04/21/how-craniosacral-therapycst-works-for-autism.

5. Harman, S., and Norton, J. (2002). Interexaminer reliability and cranial osteopathy. *Scientific Review of Alternative Medicine, 6*, 23–34.

6. National Autism Center. (2009). *The National Standards Project: Addressing the Need for Evidence Based Practice Guidelines for Autism Spectrum Disorders.* Randolph, MA: National Autism Center.

6. DAILY LIFE THERAPY

1. Quill, K., Gurry, S., and Larkin, A. (1989). Daily Life Therapy: A Japanese model for educating children with autism. *Journal of Autism and Developmental Disorders, 19*(4), 625–635.

2. Musashino Higashi Gakuen School. (n.d.). *Musashino Higashi Gakuen School.* Retrieved June 10, 2012, from www.musashino-higashi.org/english.htm.

3. Boston Higashi School (BHS). (n.d.). *Daily Life Therapy®.* Randolph, MA: Boston Higashi School. Retrieved April 10, 2012, from www.bostonhigashi.org/about.php?id=8.

4. Rugeley Horizon School. (n.d.). *Rugeley Horizon Overview.* Retrieved April 10, 2012, from www.priorygroup.com/Locations/West-Midlands/Rugeley-Horizon.aspx.

5. Larkin, A. S., and Gurry, S. (1998). Brief report: Progress reported in three children with autism using daily life therapy. *Journal of Autism and Developmental Disorders, 28*(4), 339–342.

6. www.mass.gov/anf/budget-taxes-and-procurement/oversight-agencies/osd/special-education-pricing.html.

7. DEVELOPMENTAL INDIVIDUAL-DIFFERENCE RELATIONSHIP-BASED MODEL/FLOORTIME

1. Greenspan, S. I., and Wieder, S. (2006). *Engaging Autism: Using the Floortime Approach to Help Children Relate, Communicate, and Think.* Cambridge, MA: Da Capo Lifelong Books.

2. ICDL (Interdisciplinary Council on Developmental and Learning Disorders). (n.d.). *ICDL: DIR/Floortime.* Retrieved June 10, 2012, from www.icdl.com.

3. Wieder, S., and Greenspan, S. I. (2003). Climbing the symbolic ladder in the DIR model through Floor Time/interactive play. *Autism, 7*(4), 425–435.

4. ICDL. (n.d.). *Floortime Overview.* Retrieved April 10, 2012, from www.icdl.com/dirFloortime/overview/index.shtml.

5. National Autism Center. (2009). *The National Standards Project: Addressing the Need for Evidence Based Practice Guidelines for Autism Spectrum Disorders.* Randolph, MA: National Autism Center.

6. The Early Intervention Network. (n.d.). *Enabling Families to Act Early Against Autism: Sorting Through Autism Treatments.* Retrieved April 10, 2012, from www.actearly.org/site/PageNavigator/trt_sorting_treatments.

8. DIETARY SUPPLEMENTS

1. Xia, R. R. (2011). Effectiveness of nutritional supplements for reducing symptoms in autism spectrum disorder. *Journal of Alternative and Complementary Medicine, 17*, 271–274.

2. Rossignol, D. A. (2009). Novel and emerging treatments for autism spectrum disorders: A systematic review. *Annals of Clinical Psychiatry, 21*(4), 213–236.

3. Office of Dietary Supplements (ODS). (n.d.). *Dietary Supplements: What You Need to Know.* Retrieved June 10, 2012, from http://ods.od.nih.gov/pubs/DS_WhatYouNeedToKnow.pdf.

4. Kern, J. K., Miller, V. S., Cauller, L., Kendall, R., Mehta, J., and Dodd, M. (2001). Effectiveness of N,N-Dimethylglycine in autism and pervasive developmental disorder. *Journal of Child Neurology, 16*(3), 169–173.

5. Nye, C., and Brice, A. (2009). Combined vitamin B6-magnesium treatment in autism spectrum disorder. *Cochrane Database of Systematic Reviews*, (1).

6. Amminger, G. P., Berger, G. E., Schäfer, M. R., Klier, C., Friedrich, M. H., and Feucht, M. (2007). Omega-3 fatty acids supplementation in children with autism: A double-blind randomized, placebo-controlled pilot study. *Biological Psychiatry, 61*(4), 551–553.

7. Bent, S., Bertoglio, K., and Hendren, R. L. (2009). Omega-3 fatty acids for autistic spectrum disorder: A systematic review. *Journal of Autism and Developmental Disorders, 39*(8), 1145–1154.

8. Meiri, G., Bichovsky, Y., and Belmaker, R. (2009). Omega-3 fatty acid treatment in autism. *Journal of Child and Adolescent Psychopharmacology, 19*(4), 449–451.

9. Johnson, C. R., Handen, B. L., Zimmer, M., and Sacca, K. (2010). Polyunsaturated fatty acid supplementation in young children with autism. *Journal of Developmental and Physical Disabilities, 22*, 1–10.

10. WIC (Special supplemental Nutrition Program for Women, Infants, and Children) Learning Online. (n.d.). *Harmful Supplements.* Retrieved June 10, 2012, from www.nal.usda.gov/wicworks/WIC-Learning-Online/support/job_aids/harmful.pdf.

9. GLUTEN-FREE/CASEIN-FREE DIET

1. Whiteley, P., and Shattock, P. (2002). Biochemical aspects in autism spectrum disorders: Updating the opioid-excess theory and presenting new opportunities for biomedical intervention. *Expert Opinion on Therapeutic Targets, 6*(2), 175–183.

2. Panksepp, J. (1979). A neurochemical theory of autism. *Trends in Neurosciences, 2*, 174–177.

3. Elder, J. H., Shankar, M., Shuster, J., Theriaque, D., Burns, S., and Sherrill, L. (2006). The gluten-free, casein-free diet in autism: Results of a preliminary double blind clinical trial. *Journal of Autism and Developmental Disorders, 36*(3), 413–420.

4. Mulloy, A., Lang, R., O'Reilly, M., Sigafoos, J., Lancioni, G., and Rispoli, M. (2011). Addendum to "gluten-free and casein-free diets in treatment of autism spectrum disorders: A systematic review." *Research in Autism Spectrum Disorders, 5*(1), 86–88.

5. Arnold, G. L., Hyman, S. L., Mooney, R. A., and Kirby, R. S. (2003). Plasma amino acids profiles in children with autism. *Journal of Autism and Developmental Disorders, 33*, 449–454.

6. Heiger, M. L., England, L. J., Molloy, C. A., Yu, K. F., Manning-Courtney, P., and Mills, J. L. (2008). Reduced bone cortical thickness in boys with autism or autism spectrum disorders. *Journal of Autism and Developmental Disorders, 38*, 848–856.

7. National Autism Center. (2009). *The National Standards Project: Addressing the Need for Evidence Based Practice Guidelines for Autism Spectrum Disorders.* Randolph, MA: National Autism Center.

10. HYPERBARIC OXYGEN THERAPY

1. WoundSource. (n.d.). *FDA Approved Uses for Hyperbaric Oxygen Therapy.* Retrieved April 5, 2012, from www.woundsource.com/blog/fda-approved-uses-hyperbaric-oxygen-therapy.

2. Gill, A., and Bell, C. (2004). Hyperbaric oxygen: Its uses, mechanisms of action and outcomes. *QJM, 97*, 385–395.

3. Oxford Hyperbaric Oxygen Therapy Center. (n.d.). *Autism.* Retrieved April 24, 2012, from www.healingwithhbot.com/autism.asp.

4. Rossignol, D. (2007). Hyperbaric oxygen therapy might improve certain pathophysiological findings in autism. *Medical Hypotheses, 68*(6), 1208–1227.

5. Association for Science in Autism Treatment (ASAT). (n.d.). *Hyperbaric Oxygen Therapy.* Retrieved June 10, 2012, from www.asatonline.org/treatment/treatments/hyperb.htm.

6. Saft, G. (2005). *Hyperbaric Oxygen Healing: What is HBOT and How Can It Help?* Retrieved June 10, 2012, from www.hyperbaric-oxygen-ca.com.

7. Johns Hopkins Neuroimmunopathology Laboratory. (n.d.). *FAQs: The Meaning of Neuroinflammatory Findings in Autism.* Retrieved June 10, 2012, from www.neuro.jhmi.edu/neuroimmunopath/autism_faqs.htm.

8. Rossignol, D., and Rossignol, L. (2006). Hyperbaric oxygen therapy may improve symptoms in autistic children. *Medical Hypotheses, 67*(2), 216–228.

9. Rossignol, D. A., Rossignol, L. W., James, S. J., Melnyk, S., and Mumper, E. (2007). The effects of hyperbaric oxygen therapy on oxidative stress, inflammation, and symptoms in children with autism: An open-label pilot study. *BMC Pediatrics, 7*(1), 36.

10. Rossignol, D. A., Rossignol, L. W., Smith, S., Schneider, C., *et al.* (2009). Hyperbaric treatment for children with autism: A multicenter, randomized, double-blind, controlled trial. *BMC Pediatrics, 9*(1), 21.

11. Granpeesheh, D., Tarbox, J., Dixon, D. R., Wilke, A. E., Allen, M. S., and Bradstreet, J. J. (2010). Randomized trial of hyperbaric oxygen therapy for children with autism. *Research in Autism Spectrum Disorders, 4*(2), 268–275.

12. Jepson, B., Granpeesheh, D., Tarbox, J., Olice, M., *et al.* (2011). Controlled evaluation of the effects of hyperbaric oxygen therapy on the behavior of 16 children with autism spectrum disorders. *Journal of Autism and Developmental Disorders, 41*, 575–588.

11. THE MILLER METHOD

1. Miller, A., and Eller-Miller, E. (2000). The Miller Method: A cognitive-developmental systems approach for children with body organization, social, and communication issues. In S. Greenspan and D. Weider (eds) *The ICDL Clinical Practice Guidelines Redefining the Standards of Care for Infants, Children, and Families with Special Needs.* Bethesda, MD: Interdisciplinary Council on Developmental and Learning Disorders.

2. Miller, A., and Miller, E. E. (1973). Cognitive-developmental training with elevated boards and sign language. *Journal of Autism and Childhood Schizophrenia, 3*(1), 65–85.

3. Miller, A. (n.d.). *The Miller Method: For Children with Autism Spectrum and Severe Learning Disorders.* Retrieved June 10, 2012, from http://millermethod.org.

4. Cook, C. E. (1998). The Miller Method: A case study illustrating use of the approach with children in autism in interdisciplinary settings. *Journal of Developmental and Learning Disorders, 2*(2), 231–264.

12. MUSIC THERAPY

1. American Music Therapy Association (AMTA). (n.d.). *Music Therapy Fact Sheets and Bibliographies.* Retrieved April 5, 2012, from www.musictherapy.org/research/factsheets.

2. Wimpory, D. C., Chadwick, P., and Nash, S. (1995). Brief report. Musical Interaction Therapy for children with autism: An evaluative case study with two-year follow-up. *Journal of Autism and Developmental Disorders, 25*(5), 541–552.

3. Evers, S. (1992). Music Therapy in the treatment of autistic children: Medico-sociological data from the Federal Republic of Germany. *Acta Paedopsychiatrica, 55,* 157–158.

4. Whipple, J. (2004). Music in intervention for children and adolescents with autism: A meta-analysis. *Journal of Music Therapy, 41,* 90–106.

5. Boso, M., Emanuele, E., Minazzi, V., Abbamonte, M., and Politi, P. (2007). Effect of long-term interactive music therapy on behavior profile and musical skills in young adults with severe autism. *Journal of Alternative and Complementary Medicine, 13*(7), 709–712.

6. Kim, J., Wigram, T., and Gold, C. (2008). The effects of Improvisational Music Therapy on joint attention behaviors in autistic children: A randomized controlled study. *Journal of Autism and Developmental Disorders, 38*(9), 1758–1766.

7. National Autism Center. (2009). *The National Standards Project: Addressing the Need for Evidence Based Practice Guidelines for Autism Spectrum Disorders.* Randolph, MA: National Autism Center.

13. P.L.A.Y. PROJECT HOME CONSULTATION PROGRAM

1. Greenspan, S. I., and Wieder, S. (1997). Developmental patterns and outcomes in infants and children with disorders in relating and communicating: A chart review of 200 cases of children with autistic spectrum diagnoses. *Journal of Developmental and Learning Disorders, 1,* 87–141.

2. Solomon, R., Necheles, J., Ferch, C., and Bruckman, D. (2007). Pilot study of a parent training program for young children with autism: The PLAY Project Home Consultation program. *Autism, 11*(3), 205–224.

3. National Autism Center. (2009). *The National Standards Project: Addressing the Need for Evidence Based Practice Guidelines for Autism Spectrum Disorders.* Randolph, MA: National Autism Center.

14. RELATIONSHIP DEVELOPMENT INTERVENTION

1. Gutstein, S. E., and Sheeley, R. K. (2002). *Relationship Development Intervention with Young Children: Social and Emotional Development Activities for Asperger Syndrome, Autism, PDD and NLD.* London: Jessica Kingsley.

2. Capps, L., Kasari, C., Yirmiya, N., and Sigman, M. (1993). Parental perception of emotional expressiveness in children with autism. *Journal of Consulting and Clinical Psychology, 61*(3), 475–484.

3. Minshew, N. J., Sweeney, J., and Luna, B. (2002). Autism as a selective disorder of complex information processing and underdevelopment of neocortical systems. *Molecular Psychiatry, 7*, S14–S15.

4. Gutstein, S. E., Burgess, A. F., and Montfort, K. (2007). Evaluation of the Relationship Development Intervention Program. *Autism, 11*(5), 397–411.

5. National Autism Center. (2009). *The National Standards Project: Addressing the Need for Evidence Based Practice Guidelines for Autism Spectrum Disorders.* Randolph, MA: National Autism Center.

15. SENSORY INTEGRATION THERAPY

1. Ayres, A. J. (1972). *Sensory Integration and Learning Disorders.* Los Angeles, CA: Western Psychological Services.

2. Schaaf, R. C., and Miller, L. J. (2005). Occupational therapy using a sensory integrative approach for children with developmental disabilities. *Mental Retardation and Developmental Disabilities Research Reviews, 11*(2), 143–148.

3. Dawson, G., and Watling, R. (2000). Interventions to facilitate auditory, visual, and motor integration in autism: A review of the evidence. *Journal of Autism and Developmental Disorders, 30*, 415–421.

4. Pfeiffer, B. A., Koenig, K., Kinnealey, M., Sheppard, M., and Henderson, L. (2011). Research Scholars Initiative. Effectiveness of sensory integration interventions in children with autism spectrum disorders: A pilot study. *American Journal of Occupational Therapy, 65*, 76–85.

5. National Autism Center. (2009). *The National Standards Project: Addressing the Need for Evidence Based Practice Guidelines for Autism Spectrum Disorders.* Randolph, MA: National Autism Center.

6. American Academy of Pediatrics. (2001). Technical report: The pediatrician's role in the diagnosis and management of Autistic Spectrum Disorder in children. *Pediatrics, 107*(5), E85–E85.

7. Healing Thresholds. (n.d.). *Autism Therapy: Sensory Integration.* Retrieved April 5, 2012, from http://autism.healingthresholds.com/therapy/sensory-integration.

16. THE SON-RISE PROGRAM

1. Autism Treatment Center of America. (n.d.). *The Son-Rise Program.* Retrieved June 10, 2012, from www.autismtreatmentcenter.org.

2. Kaufman, B. N. (1976). *Son-Rise.* New York: Harper & Row.

3. Kaufman, B. N. (1994). *Son-Rise: The Miracle Continues.* Tiburon, CA: H. J. Kramer.

4. National Autism Center. (2009). *The National Standards Project: Addressing the Need for Evidence Based Practice Guidelines for Autism Spectrum Disorders.* Randolph, MA: National Autism Center.

17. TEACCH

1. University of North Carolina, Chapel Hill. (2006). *Division TEACCH.* Retrieved August 8, 2012 from http://teacch.com/about-us-1/what-is-teacch.

2. Schopler, E., Mesibov, G. B., and Hearsey, K. (1995). Structured teaching in the TEACCH system. In E. Schopler and G. B. Mesibov (eds) *Learning and Cognition in Autism.* New York: Plenum Press.

3. Autism-PDD.Net. (n.d.). *Using TEACCH for Autism Treatment.* Retrieved April 15, 2012, from www.autism-pdd.net/teacch.html.

4. Mesibov, G. B., and Shea, V. (2010). The TEACCH Program in the era of evidence-based practice. *Journal of Autism and Developmental Disorders, 40*(5), 570–579.

5. Panerai, S., Zingale, M., Trubia, G., Finocchiaro, M., *et al.* (2009). Special education versus inclusive education: The role of the TEACCH Program. *Journal of Autism and Developmental Disorders, 39*(6), 874–882.

6. Panerai, S., Ferrante, L., Caputo, V., and Impellizzeri, C. (1998). Use of structured teaching for treatment of children with autism and severe and profound mental retardation. *Education and Training in Mental Retardation and Developmental Disabilities, 33*, 367–374.

7. Tsang, S. M., Shek, D. L., Lam, L. L., Tang, F. Y., and Cheung, P. P. (2007). Brief Report. Application of the TEACCH Program on Chinese pre-school children with autism: Does culture make a difference? *Journal of Autism and Developmental Disorders, 37*(2), 390–396.

8. National Autism Center. (2009). *The National Standards Project: Addressing the Need for Evidence Based Practice Guidelines for Autism Spectrum Disorders.* Randolph, MA: National Autism Center.

Index